FAKING IT

FAKING IT

U.S. Hegemony in a "Post-Phallic" Era

CYNTHIA WEBER

UNIVERSITY OF MINNESOTA PRESS

Minneapolis • London

The University of Minnesota Press gratefully acknowledges permission to reprint parts of the following essays. Portions of chapter 4 appeared as "Shoring Up a Sea of Signs: How the Caribbean Basin Initiative Framed the United States' Invasion of Grenada," in *Environment and Planning D: Society and Space* 12 (5) (December 1994): 547–58; reprinted with permission of the publisher, Pion Limited, London. Portions of chapter 5 appeared as "Something's Missing: Male Hysteria and the U.S. Invasion of Panama," in *Genders* 19 (spring 1994): 171–97; reprinted with permission of New York University Press. Portions of chapter 6 appeared as "Masquerading and the U.S.-Led 'Intervasion' of Haiti," first published in *Sovereignty and Subjectivity*, edited by Jenny Edkins, Nalini Persram, and Veronique Pin-fat, copyright 1998 by Lynne Rienner Publishers, Inc.; reprinted with permission of the publisher.

Published by the University of Minnesota Press
111 Third Avenue South, Suite 290
Minneapolis, MN 55401-2520
http://www.upress.umn.edu

Library of Congress Cataloging-in-Publication Data

Weber, Cynthia.
Faking it : U.S. hegemony in a "post-phallic" era / Cynthia Weber.
p.   cm.
Includes bibliographical references (p.   ) and index.
ISBN 0-8166-3269-3 (hc : alk. paper). — ISBN 0-8166-3270-7 (pb : alk. paper)
1. Caribbean Area—Foreign relations—United States. 2. United States—Foreign relations—Caribbean Area. 3. United States—Foreign relations—1945–1989. 4. United States—Foreign relations—1989–   5. International relations—Psychological aspects. 6. Masculinity—Political aspects. 7. Feminism. 8. Feminist theory. I. Title.
F2178.U6W43   1999
327.730729—dc21
98-40327

Printed in the United States of America on acid-free paper

The University of Minnesota is an equal-opportunity educator and employer.

11 10 09 08 07 06 05 04 03 02 01 00 99   10 9 8 7 6 5 4 3 2 1

For M/Z

... the best strategy for challenging the phallic
authority of the penis is *laughter*...

—*Elizabeth Grosz*

PREFACE

This book has already sparked many reactions. They began with a draft of the Panama chapter that I was invited to write for an edited volume on discursive readings of international relations. Upon reading the draft, the editors promptly "uninvited" the essay. I then sent the essay off to the journal *Signs*, and a reviewer responded by labeling me an "unconscionable feminist." It was Ann Kibbey, the editor of *Genders*, who—faced with polarized reviews—rang me up and asked me the critical question, "Is the essay meant to be funny?" "Yes," I assured her, "but it is more than that. It is supposed to be a strategic use of humor to make critical intellectual points about U.S. hegemony, psychoanalytic theory, and dichotomous representations of sex, gender, and sexuality." Ann gave me the chance to revise the essay, which she published ("Something's Missing: Male Hysteria and the U.S. Invasion of Panama," *Genders* 19 [spring 1994]: 171–97). A version of the essay was later reprinted in Marysia Zalewski and Jane Parpart's edited volume *The "Man" Question in International Relations* (Boulder, Colo.: Westview Press, 1998).

The mixed reactions to this work continued. A very different version of my reading of the Grenada invasion was invited to appear in a volume of *Society and Space* guest-edited by Simon Dalby and Gerard Toal and edited by Geraldine Pratt ("Shoring Up a Sea of Signs:

How the Caribbean Basin Initiative Framed the United States' Invasion of Grenada," *Environment and Planning D: Society and Space* 12 (5) [December 1994]: 547–58). Similarly, I was invited by Jenny Edkins, Nalini Persram, and Veronique Pin-fat to participate in a conference they organized and to contribute an earlier draft of my Haiti chapter to their resulting edited volume ("Masquerading and the U.S.-Led 'Intervasion' of Haiti," in *Sovereignty and Subjectivity* [Boulder, Colo.: Lynne Rienner Publishers, 1998]). In contrast, a full professor from a U.S. political science department shared with me his reactions to a paper that now forms part of this volume. He wrote of the paper that it was the intellectual and moral equivalent to rap music. It was clear from his letter that he did not mean this as a compliment.

"I'm always amazed that you give these sorts of papers at conferences," a feminist colleague said to me. "Why do you think the boys want to listen to your work?" My reply was that I do not think the boys—or many of the girls—do want to listen. Presented to international relations theorists, geographers, and Caribbean specialists, these arguments over the years have provoked two general sorts of responses—either outright hostility and dismissal or the much more frequent response of audience members joining in the conversation with their own gender anecdotes. But the effect has often been the same—to make sex, gender, and sexuality studies a sideshow to the main event of "serious" theory or history. This book repackages the sideshow as the main event. It is *not* "for the boys." It is about them.

This book simplifies as much overt theory as possible in an attempt to make accessible a critical way of looking at U.S. leadership and to queer heterosexual codings of sex, gender, and sexuality. It tells one story of U.S.–Caribbean relations between 1959 and 1994. It stars an "America" that slips easily in, out, and between various sexes, genders, and sexualities. So configured, this body "stands for" many things—seldom just a U.S. citizenry acting in foreign affairs through its elected presidential administrations, almost always a self-imagined hegemonic U.S. body politic that passes in a popular U.S. imaginary as the "American body politic," and occasionally an "American body politic" that attempts to pass as "the world as we know it." Although I am careful *not* to correct these various confusions, my point is not to endorse them either. Rather, my purpose is to critically engage popular *imaginaries* of a figural "America" as well as what is simultaneously absent and present from them—queerness.

As amorphously seductive as the American body politic it describes, the term *queer* lacks definite character. It has been described as "contra-, non- or anti-straight" (Doty, 1993: xv) and as "an in-your-face rejection of the proper response to heteronormativity, a version of acting up" (Hennessy, 1993: 967). It might also be thought of as Roland Barthes thinks of the plural, as "that which *confuses* meaning, the norm, normativity" (Barthes, 1976: 109). The compelling paradox in America's story is that it is the hegemony-seeking American body politic that is "acting up" to secure its heteronormativity (something that seems surprising to all except those who view "gay male identity as the site of privileged subjectivity" [Walters, 1996: 836]).

This story errs in many ways. For narrative effect, it sets up the U.S. encounter with Castro's Cuba as the primal scene in which U.S. hegemonic power began to decline and U.S. queer strategies began to affect a straight, hegemonic masculinity. In "fact," U.S. hegemonic decline (assuming that it is "real") is multicausal and both pre- and post-dates the events of 1959. Yet it is the Castro revolution that is singled out in U.S. foreign-policy discourse as the time when things began to go irrevocably wrong in the U.S. imaginary about its "American" body politic. It is for this reason that I overplay this castrating encounter.

Another story choice is to focus almost exclusively on moments of crisis in U.S.–Caribbean relations, thus giving the impression that queer practices are not at work during times of relative calm. There are ample examples of queered U.S. subjectivity during calm periods. I choose moments of crisis for two reasons: because a general readership is more likely to be familiar with crises and because queer practices tend to be more noticeable during these periods.

My focus on U.S.–Caribbean crises also means that I have failed to analyze several U.S. administrations. Some presidents, such as Richard

Nixon, Gerald Ford, and Jimmy Carter, seem more like characters who make cameo appearances than central figures in U.S.–Caribbean relations. Yet it would be a mistake to reduce the object of my analysis — a variously *imagined* American body politic that is rhetorically circulated *by* U.S. presidents — to U.S. presidents themselves. I do trace the dissemination of queer signifiers through presidential bodies and this has the effect of queering the Bush and Clinton presidencies (Rubenstein, in progress). Even so, my objective lies elsewhere. It is to reread in a Barthesian sense the U.S. collective "national fantasy" about its hegemony, however and wherever this fantasy is configured (Barthes, 1974; Berlant, 1991). This makes my use of psychoanalytic theory necessary (to explore the unconscious) but questionable (because my object of analysis is as often collective as it is individual). Yet it is in part the play between the personal/collective and the conscious/unconscious that drives America's hegemonic quest in the Caribbean and beyond.

Finally, I pay scant attention to most Caribbean administrations caught up in this imaginary narrative of U.S. hegemony. Mine is not a Caribbean tale but a U.S. narrative, one that is very much invested in U.S. imaginary impressions of its hemispheric hegemony. *Faking It* attempts to subvert U.S. popular imaginaries about an American body politic by rethinking the categories of sex, gender, and sexuality and their relationships to U.S. hegemony.

Over the years, I have been supported in this project by more people than I can mention here. I will single out a few. My foremost intellectual debt is to my colleague at Purdue University, Diane Rubenstein. Diane gave me the confidence to write provocatively through her example and friendship. Diane's suggestion that I think about Manuel Noriega through the concept of male hysteria — something Diane had done in her own work on George Bush — was the early inspiration for this project. Her constructive criticism throughout — from suggesting the title *Faking It* to closely reading and editing chapters — immensely improved my still imperfect work. Her traces — like those of Rick Ashley — are on every page. Lyn Kathlene allowed me to follow

1. PICTURE THIS

This is the United States as I see it today—a white headless body of indecipherable sex and gender cloaked in the flag and daggered with a queer dildo harnessed to its midsection. This figure finds its global footing on Caribbean islands and its hegemonic identity reflected in the Caribbean Sea. Both foreign foundational formations—land and sea—fool the U.S. body politic that its stands for all of America. It is America's caped crusader. It is an American body politic. Cartoonlike in its heroic pose, it stands ready for action of whatever sort in whatever locale.

My ("post")hegemonic "America" emerges from a story of conquest, loss, and recovery long played out in U.S. foreign policy but one that reached a critical anticlimax in U.S.–Caribbean relations between 1959 and 1994. During this period, a masculinized United States "lost" its Caribbean reward for hemispheric valor in the Spanish-American War—the feminized Cuba, its symbolic object of desire. Playing a role in the U.S. imaginary as a sort of trophy mistress, Cuba was the near colony and certain feminine complement the United States relied on to forestall any pending midlife/hegemonic/masculine identity crisis. The United States liaison with Cuba evidenced U.S. supreme dominance in the Caribbean.

But hegemonic crisis came nonetheless, in the form of the Cuban Revolution of 1959. This revolution, led by Fidel Castro, grafted Castro's hypermasculinity onto the iconic femininity of prerevolutionary Cuba. The effect of the Cuba/Castro pairing was not to cancel out Cuba's symbolic femininity and overwrite it with a rebellious masculinity. Rather, both aspects of Cuba's gendered identity—iconic femininity and hypermasculinity—survived with a vengeance, reengendering Cuba with a mixed identity best described as a "U.S.O.—Unidentified *Sexual Object*" (BIMBOX 2; quoted in Berlant and Freeman, 1993: 221).

Misreading Castro and Castro's Cuba, the United States misrecognized the mixed gender of Cuba and continued to pursue Cuba as an idealized feminine object, even once its mistress had grown a beard. "Well, nobody's perfect" was the only reply the United States uttered to Castro's Cuba in 1959, because to say anything else would have been to bring its own hegemonic masculinity into question. But even this strategy undermined the U.S. position because the chosen object of U.S. desire was not who the U.S. hoped to see when it looked to Cuba. Cuba the trophy mistress turned out to be no trophy at all in the straight symbolic economy of U.S. foreign policy because this mistress was also a mister. Confronted with the "realities" of Cuba, the United States seemingly faced two options: either a symbolic castration—a loss of phallic power coded as an inability to produce meaning that resulted from a lack of a feminine object in which to "express" its masculine identity—or a queering/nonnormalizing of its subjectivity if it retained Cuba the U.S.O. as its object of desire (Warner, 1993: vvi–xxxi). Whether it could not find its phallus or the only phallus it could find was a fake (and eventually queer) one, the U.S. encounter with Castro's Cuba ushered the United States into a "post-phallic" era—an era in which U.S. hegemonic/phallic authority had been critically transformed.

Since its initial encounter with Castro's Cuba, the United States has been struggling to reclaim a normalized hegemonic masculinity by (re)covering its losses. As a result, U.S. policy toward the Caribbean has consisted of a series of displacements of castration or castration anxiety, some of which paradoxically affect straight hegemonic masculinity by queering U.S. subjectivity. Whereas previously the United States turned a blind eye to the "realities" of Cuba, since the 1960s the United States has avoided its own "realities," insisting on not seeing either itself as castrated or the queer compensatory strategies that enable it to appear "straight." Having originally misread Cuba, the United States now misreads itself (something it is well practiced in; see LaFeber, 1994).

Three strategies have dominated U.S. foreign policy misreadings and projections of itself toward the Caribbean in the aftermath of its encounter with Cuba: sheer denial in its invasion of the Dominican Republic that the United States ever suffered a symbolic castration; straight and queer simulations of phallic power in Grenada and Panama, respectively; and male masquerade in which the United States embraced its symbolic castration by symbolically cross-dressing in order both to guard itself against castration and to simulate phallic power as it did in Haiti. Since 1959, then, the United States has been "faking it" — "it" being a straight/normalized masculine hegemonic identity and the phallic power (ability to produce meaning that comes with such an identity.

Although the United States has been faking it in and beyond the Caribbean, its Caribbean compensations go to the "root" of the U.S. identity crisis. The Caribbean is the location to which the United States historically has turned to "find itself." For the United States, the Caribbean links "the discourse of myth with the discourse of history; or even, the discourse of resistance with the language of power" (Benítez-Rojo, 1992: 4). It is where U.S. "white rhythms," rhythms that "are narcissistic rhythms, obsessed with their own legitimation," encounter Caribbean "copper, black, and yellow rhythms." These latter rhythms, when compared to the supposedly colorless U.S. ones, "appear as turbulent and erratic,...as eruptions of gases and lava that issue from an elemental stratum, still in formation" (ibid., 26).

Although U.S. foreign policy always narrates its encounter with the Caribbean from its own standpoint — reading myth through history and resistance through power—it is the tension generated from the encounter of contradictory narratives that defy synthesis that makes the U.S. story possible; for without the Caribbean narratives of myth and resistance, U.S. foreign policy narratives of the region would be those of the automatic march of time and the use of power for its own sake. "[A]n argument that sees in the biological, economic, and cultural whitening of Caribbean society a series of successive steps toward 'progress' " (ibid.) requires some place, people, and time at/ on/in which its story may unfold. The United States requires the Caribbean in order to be itself.

The link between U.S. hegemonic identity and Caribbean stability is at least as old as the Monroe Doctrine, an 1823 proclamation by President Monroe linking U.S. security with a hemispheric system of governance free of monarchical power or further colonization by European monarchies. The president declared, "The political system of the allied power [of Europe known as the Holy Alliance] is essentially different... from that of America.... [W]e should consider any attempt on their part to extend their system to any portion of this hemisphere as dangerous to our peace and safety " (quoted in Chayes, 1974: 116).

Mixed with various corollaries over the years and mythologized into a strategic doctrine that long outlived the Holy Alliance against which it was aimed, the Monroe Doctrine has become a vital aspect of the "Americas myth." This myth holds, among other things, that "[t]he Western Hemisphere is the geographic *tabula rasa* on which God (Providence, History) demonstrates civilization's advance through agents understood to be the descendants of Europeans"; that "[t]he content of this advance is freedom and progress"; and that "[t]he United States of America is where this project first began and where it still excels" (Kenworthy, 1995: 18). Because, in the U.S. view, the "United States is the vanguard of a hemisphere that, following its leadership, is a vanguard region of the world" (ibid.), instability in the Caribbean Basin, the myth continues, may constrain U.S. global performance and the U.S. ability to act as a world power, a world leader, a global hegemon.

If only the "whirlpool" (Pastor, 1992) that is the Caribbean could be calmed into a tranquil reflective/projecting surface — into a "faithful, polished mirror" (Irigaray, 1985a: 27) or stable screen — then this femininely engendered Caribbean Sea turned U.S. pond could dutifully reflect/simulate U.S. subjectivity as hegemonically masculine.

In its search for hegemonic masculinity, the American body politic's Caribbean compensations often parallel its non-Caribbean concerns. Caribbean cases could be paired with other U.S. concerns, reading, for example, the Cuban case in the context of the Cold War generally, the Dominican invasion as "Vietnam writ small" (Wiarda, 1975: 835), Grenada as a simulated success in light of the failures in Lebanon and Nicaragua, Panama as a preface to the Persian Gulf War, and Haiti as a diplomatic success to balance out the diplomatic failures in Bosnia. In this regard, a Caribbean context connects without canceling out the various disjointed gestures of the United States to assert its global hegemonic identity, even as hegemonic identity (like all identity) becomes increasingly illusory.

The trauma of U.S. hegemonic loss — and various guises used to overcome it — are expressed in my imaginary image of America. America's body politic has been decapitated. Headlessness marks its Caribbean castration. As Marjorie Garber reminds us, "in . . . the logic behind Freud's reading of the Medusa, 'face' and 'penis' become symbolic alternatives for one another" (1992: 247). Losing one's head, then, is the symbolic equivalent of losing (the function of) one's penis and the phallic power that is supposed to accompany it. Left headless and thus voiceless, the United States no longer can be assured the last word in global affairs. Its self-appointed international role as keeper and enforcer of the law of the father is now in jeopardy.

Additionally, this faceless figure allows — indeed, insists on — a slippage between some imaginary America and a dual notion of Americans (U.S. citizens and hemispheric citizens). Lauren Berlant suggests that "the experience of identity might be personal and private, but its forms are always 'collective' and political" (1991: 3). The unoccupied space at the top of this torso is reminiscent of a carnival cutout that instructs the user to "put your head here." America's body politic can and must be worn by every American—U.S. and other—for an imaginary America constructs the identities of all Americans but seemingly belongs to no American in particular. This is among the ways in which the hegemonic reach of the United States appears to be benign. America's Caribbean traumas, then, are traumas experienced by every American in the hemisphere.

When putting on America's imaginary body, Americans blend into the supposedly colorless corporeality of the United States—whiteness, a hegemonic hue that is "everything and nothing...[and that] both disappears behind and is subsumed into other identities" (Dyer, 1988: 45–46). Over their transparent tinge, they dress themselves in the U.S. flag. Yet this latter mark of patriotism crosses out/over the mark of gender. Clothed in the flag, Americans participate in "a masquerade that smudges the clarity of gender" (Berlant and Freeman, 1993: 193) for their individual bodies and for the American body politic. What is the gender of the American body politic? This is undecidable. It is a mystery draped in a flag. The flag functions as a veil that conceals America's bodily "facts." Unlike the Lacanian veil that ensures the potency of the phallus, the U.S. flag worn as "dress" red, white, and blue unveils a question—does America have the phallus?

This question arises from another slip, this time between flag and fag. This figure of America is costumed for *international* action, standing as it is on Caribbean islands, ready to execute its duties in some foreign locale. The presumption of gendered readings of international politics has long been that sovereign bodies acting in international affairs are male (Elshtain, 1987). Read through that supposition, this American body is in drag. It is not just any caped crusader but a man in a dress. As such, it is doubly marked by both the presence of the phallus (this is a man who has a penis and therefore could wield the phallus) and the absence of the phallus (this is a man in a *dress*). Although male cross-dressing and homosexuality need not imply one another, in the United States male transvestites very often are called fags, a term connoting a dephallusized other. The leaps in logic bound up in this series of assumptions about the international display of the U.S. f(l)ag seem to be tailor-made for the observation that "the radical spectacle of the body's rendezvous with the flag has seemed to yoke unlike things together" (Berlant and Freeman, 1993: 220).

Which brings us to the "yoke" of another sort that joins together the flag and a silicone supplement. Our caution as to a queer reading of this figure now seems to be inappropriate for the American body politic has strapped on a lavender dildo. As the Queer Nation colored map of the United States reminds us, red, white and blue blend to produce lavender, "a shocking new shade of queer" (ibid., 205). This strategic harnessing of queer sexuality at the intersections of America's global and sexual identities (re)covers America's international phallic power while at the same time throwing its normalized masculine hegemonic identity into crisis. America's body politic seems to accept its symbolic castration and proudly displays the "adjustment" it has made that readies it for international action. In so doing, it boldly returns the question of its own phallic power, daring international others to guess as to the status and function of its member(s).

Yet it is critically important what the American body politic's acceptance of its symbolic castration does not accept, what a rephallusized United States must not recognize—the queerness of its "member." This is precisely what the turbulent history of U.S.–Caribbean relations threatens to reveal; for while U.S. foreign policy attempts to calm the Caribbean region—to stabilize it by feminizing it so it can act as a tranquil reflective surface or projection screen in/onto which the United States might see its hegemonic masculinity reflected/simulated back to it—the Caribbean resists these stabilizing attempts. Whether this is by revolutionary upheavals, the introduction of foreign/communist elements, or the unpredictable mixing of colors, contexts, and challenges to U.S. policies, the Caribbean Sea as the Caribbean "See" (mirror) or "Screen" (surface for projection) always reveals more than the United States wishes to notice.

Both what the United States longs to discover and what the Caribbean Sea/See/Screen offers up for viewing are expressed in my imaginary image of America. What the United States recognizes in the Caribbean is its own hegemonic image mirrored/projected back to it. This is represented in the individual reflection/simulation of each of the colors of the U.S. flag, colors that do not run in the U.S. imaginary of the Caribbean Sea/See/Screen as a passive surface but that do run on the American body politic to create the lavender dildo. In its imaginary, the United States can use queer strategies to rephallusize itself without ever having to "come out" to itself.

But notice the edge of this reflection/simulation — where the U.S. f(l)ag meets the Caribbean Sea/See/Screen. Here the "real" that the United States must exclude in order to remain hegemonic is mirrored/projected back to it. On this viewing, the Caribbean Sea/See/Screen is not a passive surface. Rather, it disrupts U.S. hegemony because it confronts the United States with the horror of the visible, the horror of the real, the horror of its own lack and strapped-on queer accessory.

Faking It fleshes out the story this picture tells. It does so by foregrounding the figural aspects of recent U.S.–Caribbean relations, specifically as they are related to sex, gender, and sexuality. In so doing, it embodies profane treatments of "honorable" institutions (such as the presidency) and humorous analyses of "dishonorable" acts (bloody military interventions read as rapes). Yet the political implications of this reading should not be overlooked. By attending to these aspects of U.S. foreign policy discourse, *Faking It* focuses on a neglected feature of what enables events such as military interventions to occur and what their effects are on institutions such as the presidency and engendered representations of hegemonic subjectivity. It is not meant to divert attention away from other political implications of these foreign policy discourses; rather, in accordance with feminist readings of politics, it attempts to explode the very notion of politics through a strategic use of laughter.

As Mikhail Bakhtin noted, "Laughter liberates not only from external censorship but first of all from the great interior censor" (quoted in Edelman, 1988: 128). Laughter defamiliarizes discourses and events for their readers, giving readers license to disobey common expectations about what meanings a given text ought to generate. Attention is drawn to subtexts and double meanings embedded in texts. By "liberating" the interpretation of a text from the sole domain of its author's intentions, texts are remotivated with plural interpretations. Reading U.S. hegemony in this way is an attempt to illustrate "how feminists may read patriarchal texts against the grain, so that they may be actively worked upon and *strategically harnessed* for purposes for which they were not intended" (Grosz, 1995: 142; my emphasis).

2. Cas/ztro's Cuba and the Contagion of Castration

If there is a single image in the American imaginary that captures the virility of Fidel Castro, it is the photograph of him that accompanied Herbert Matthews's three-part *New York Times* series in 1957 on Castro's struggle to overthrow the government of General Fulgencio Batista. In the photo, the youthful Castro is simultaneously presented and concealed from his viewer. While the camera captures Castro's image, it also conjures up an aura of mystery and intrigue about him, affected by the shaded area in which he is standing, his unmanicured beard, and his olive fatigues and cap. The photo is cropped so that Castro's legs are not visible, making the focus of the photo Castro's broad chest. In case his military uniform and manly stature are not sufficient to underscore Castro's masculinity, Castro holds across his body a large rifle. This prop transforms his image from one of masculinity to hypermasculinity — from the mere signifier of masculinity to an oversaturation of signs of the masculine. Even Castro's gaze is masculine. Staring off into the distance wearing a stony, determined, brutish expression on his face, he is ready for anything.

Because the photograph appeared on the front page of the *New York Times,* it is tempting to read it as simply a visual accompaniment to a news story. Yet the adornments to the photo offer up clues as to other ways it might be read. Castro's autographing of the photo suggests that it might be a publicity shot. On this reading, Castro is the rising star and the American public his adoring fans, just as they were on his prior revolutionary fund-raising trip to America. Castro's inscription of the photograph, "Sierra Maestra, Febrero 17 de 1957," marks the photo as a significant historical moment. Labeled with both place and date, the photo situates Castro as a fighter on the verge of great things in an atmosphere of extreme danger at a time when Batista had declared him dead. What the photo as well as the three-part serialized telling of the Castro-led upheaval accentuate are less news than story. Castro's Cuba offers an American viewing and reading public a gripping tale, one the photo eclipses from the news. This is readily apparent in Matthews's description of Castro's photo; for it cannot contain or limit the power of the image and the symbolic context the photo implies for U.S.–Cuban relations.

Matthews's words are but hollow echoings of the story presented by Castro's image. Matthews writes of Castro: "The personality of the man is overpowering. It was easy to see that his men adored him and also to see why he has caught the imagination of the youth of Cuba all over the island. Here was an educated, dedicated fanatic, a man of ideals, of courage and of remarkable qualities of leadership" (*New York Times*, February 24, 1957). As a U.S. embassy official in Cuba put it in 1958, "In Santiago de Cuba, Fidel Castro and his 26 of July Movement are anything and everything to anyone and everyone" (Oscar H. Guerra, February 21, 1958; *FRUS 1958–1960*, 6: 34). Here, in other words, is a hero of mythical proportions. In 1959, National Security Adviser Allen Dulles believed "Castro considered himself the man on horseback, destined not only to liberate Cuba but to liberate all of the other dictatorships in Latin America." (February 12, 1959; ibid., 5: 398). In the United States in the late 1950s, this is how Fidel Castro's image was consumed. As one historian noted,

> when Fidel Castro first appeared in news magazines and on television, he could easily be seen here [in the United States] as a reappearance of the Man on Horseback, alternatively an idealist of the Brando/Zapata type or a "strong man",

like so many others who had arrived at power through coups dubbed "revolutions". Despite considerable evidence that the Cuban revolutionary war was a Latin American revolution of a new type, these two stereotypes of the idealistic "bearded fanatic" and the macho "bearded *caudillo*" persisted well into 1959. (Gosse, 1993: 45)

What so troubled the Eisenhower administration in the late 1950s was not Castro's "bearded fanaticism" or "caudilloism." The United States had long tolerated such qualities in Latin American leaders. These familiar stereotypes comforted U.S. policymakers. What threatened them was what they did not know about Castro and Castro's Cuba, what, as Matthews was to imply some years later, no one could know: "[N]o one knows the Cuban Revolution who does not know Fidel Castro. Yet his is a character of such complexity, such contradictions, such emotionalism, such irrationality, such unpredictability that no one can really know him" (Matthews, 1961: 149). Nearly a year after Castro took power, all that a U.S. Special National Intelligence Estimate could be sure of was that Fidel Castro was a "disruption of things traditional in Cuba" (December 29, 1959; *FRUS, 1958–1960*, 6: 418). What the administration could not determine was the "nature" of Castro's disruption. Was he a communist or just a nationalist? Was he anti–United States or simply neutral toward the United States? These were the types of questions that preoccupied the Eisenhower administration.

The comments of Vice President Richard Nixon on Castro offer insights both as to the character of the man and as to the missteps U.S. foreign policy was bound to make because of its reaction to Castro. After meeting with Castro in April 1959, Nixon wrote, "My own appraisal of him as a man is somewhat mixed." Castro "has those indefinable qualities which make him a leader of men" and "because he has the power to lead...we have no choice but at least to try to *orient* him in the right direction" (April 25, 1959; ibid., 6: 476; my emphasis).

It is not just Nixon's assessment of Castro that is mixed. Castro—and especially Castro's Cuba—is a mixed figure. Castro's Cuba is a location where unlike qualities are joined but not blended, where, for example, the hypermasculinity of Castro is grafted onto the iconic femininity of Cuba and where the Kennedy administration experienced its greatest foreign-policy success (Cuban missile crisis) and its worst foreign-policy blunder (Bay of Pigs invasion). Trying to "orient" such a mixed figure is always an experience that is bound to fail, an experience that inevitably leads to the orienter's own disorientation.

There is no better interpretive guide for retelling the tale of the U.S. wooing of and later disgust with Castro's Cuba than Roland Barthes's *S/Z*, which retells Honoré de Balzac's story "Sarrasine." A story of mystery, intrigue, and seduction, "Sarrasine" offers its readers mixed characters and mixed plots. In *S/Z*, Barthes does not simply reread "Sarrasine." He instructs readers (and writers) as to what reading is about. Barthes's conviction of reading is that "what is told is always the 'telling.' Ultimately, the narrative has no *object*: the narrative concerns only itself: *the narrative tells itself*" (Barthes, 1974: 213; emphasis in original). The story Barthes tells of "Sarrasine" is one that does not solve the mysteries the story presents but rather one that highlights how Balzac's story pluralizes these mysteries by locating them in relation to a figure beyond orientation—a castrato. As various characters attempt to orient themselves in relation to the castrato, each becomes disoriented and disempowered. Or, as Barthes puts it, "Castration is contagious" (ibid., 66).

The story I retell of U.S.–Cuban relations—and of U.S.–Caribbean relations more generally—begins with the failed seduction of a mixed figure (Castro's Cuba) and results in the symbolic castration of the United States—a loss of phallic power (read more generally as an inability for the United States to be guaranteed the last word in regional affairs) resulting from a lack of a normalized feminine object in which to "express" its masculinity. As it is told by the United States, these aspects of the U.S.–Cuban story are missing. By retelling this story, I both restore these vital elements to the story and demonstrate what is at stake in the U.S. misreading of the Cuba situation. As in "Sarrasine," the U.S. misreading proves to be fatal, at least for a U.S.

straight/normalized notion of masculinity in its Caribbean affairs and the hegemonic power that comes with it.

Sarras/zine

"Sarrasine" tells the story of a tale told about its title character — a young French male sculptor "kept...in total ignorance of the facts of life" (Balzac, 1974: 236) — and his involvement with La Zambinella, a mysterious figure whose past holds the key to the fortunes of a Parisian family. Sarrasine's story is told at a party by a man to a woman who has promised herself to him for the night if he solves the mystery of their host's fortune. But this is a promise the woman cannot keep. On hearing Sarrasine's story, the woman declares, "You have given me a disgust for life and for passions that will last a long time" (ibid., 253). Sarrasine's story, like Balzac's tale "Sarrasine," is the story of a failed seduction, a failure that results from an initial misreading of La Zambinella. This is Sarrasine's story.

Having finished his apprenticeship in Paris, Sarrasine leaves for Italy in 1758 to pursue his career, and, shortly after his arrival, goes to an opera where he falls in love with La Zambinella, the prima donna of the stage. La Zambinella is an "ideal beauty"(ibid., 238). To Sarrasine she displays "united, living, and delicate, those exquisite female forms he so ardently desired, of which a sculptor is at once the severest and the most passionate judge" (ibid.). "This was more than a woman, this was a masterpiece!" (ibid.). Sarrasine decides he must have La Zambinella's love and declares to himself "To be loved by her, or to die!" (ibid., 238–39).

Encouraged by La Zambinella's "eloquent glances," Sarrasine concludes that he is loved and embarks on a formal wooing of his mistress, even after being warned off by a stranger. Sarrasine cannot be dissuaded from his passion for La Zambinella. He drunkenly makes his bid for La Zambinella one evening, but his mistress escapes. On an outing to the countryside the next morning, La Zambinella refuses Sarrasine's request that she tell him that she loves him. Describing herself as "an accursed creature" in need of "a brother, a protector," La Zambinella warns Sarrasine, "I forbid you to love me. I can be your devoted friend . . . but no more" (ibid., 246–47). "Not love you!" Sarrasine exclaims. "But my dearest angel you are my life, my happiness!" To this La Zambinella inquires of Sarrasine, "And if I were not a woman?" Sarrasine thinks La Zambinella is joking, explaining to her that his artist's eye could not be deceived about such things; for, of La Zambinella, Sarrasine thinks, "This is woman herself" (ibid., 248).

Because La Zambinella refuses to give her love to Sarrasine, Sarrasine resolves to take it from her. He devises a plan to kidnap her from a party that evening, where he sees La Zambinella singing dressed like a man. Curious as to La Zambinella's appearance, Sarrasine asks a nobleman if she is so attired out of respect for the clergy present, to which the nobleman replies, "She? What she? . . . Are you joking? Where are you from? Has there ever been a woman on the Roman stage? And don't you know about the creatures who sing female roles in the Papal States? I am the one, monsieur, who gave Zambinella his voice" (ibid., 250). Sarrasine is now confronted with "a horrid truth" — the truth of the she/he — and yet it is a truth he cannot accept. "It is a woman," Sarrasine says to himself, trying to persuade himself that he alone knows the truth of La Zambinella (ibid., 251).

Sarrasine and his friends proceed with the kidnapping of La Zambinella, even though it has now been recoded from an act of love to an act of discovery and vengeance. Back in his studio, Sarrasine insists to La Zambinella, "I should kill you . . . You are nothing. If you were a man or a woman, I would kill you, but. . . . Isn't leaving you alive condemning you to something worse than death?" (ibid., 252). He then confronts the statue he has made of La Zambinella and declares, "And it's an illusion" (ibid.).

In utter despair, Sarrasine tells La Zambinella that "she" has dragged him down to "her" level. "I shall forever think of this imaginary woman when I see a real woman," he says as he gestures to the statue. "I shall always have the memory of a celestial harpy who thrusts its talons into all my manly feelings, and who will stamp all other women with a seal of imperfection! Monster! You who can give life to nothing. For me, you have wiped women from the earth!" (ibid.). Sarrasine then tries to destroy his statue of La Zambinella and to kill La Zambinella. But three men enter who rescue La Zambinella by stabbing Sarrasine in the name of La Zambinella's benefactor. "It is a good deed worthy of a Christian," Sarrasine tells his murderers as he dies. By blessing his murderers, Sarrasine transforms his murder into a suicide, thus fulfilling his promise to himself, "To be loved by her [La Zambinella], or to die!" (Barthes, 1974: 205; Balzac, 1974: 238–39).

Barthes's book *S/Z* rereads "Sarrasine." Rather than attempting to arrive at "the" singular meaning of the story, Barthes asks what pluralizes this text—what opens it to any number of different yet equally valid readings. His answer is that the plurality of the text is to be found in its telling by both its writer and its readers. Whereas the author initially pluralizes a text by, for example, giving it an intertextual relationship to other texts and cultural referents, a reader may also pluralize a text in the reading of it. Readers may approach texts not as readerly (as completed stories that they may accept or reject) but as writerly (as works in process that, on every rereading, are actively coproduced or coauthored by their readers). Readers of writerly texts interpret them. "To interpret a text is not to give it a . . . meaning, but on the contrary to appreciate what *plural* constitutes it" (Barthes, 1974: 5; emphasis in original).

Appreciating the plural of a text involves rejecting the classical privileging of a denotative or literal reading of a text over a connotative or figurative reading. This is a necessary rejection because, as Barthes suggests, connotation as well as denotation coproduce a text and its meanings. The meaning of a text can never be confined to its literal meaning or to what its author intends. Texts should not be reduced to the individuality of any author, but rather should be restored to their function (ibid., 3). "Functionally, connotation, releasing the double meaning on principle, corrupts the purity of communications: it is a deliberate 'static,' painstakingly elaborated, introduced into the fictive dialogue between author and reader, in short, a countercommunication" (ibid., 9).

I propose to reread U.S.–Cuban relations functionally, as communication and countercommunication, as denotation and connotation. In this story as in any other, "denotation is not the first [or originary] meaning, but it pretends to be so . . . it is . . . the superior myth by which the text pretends to return to the nature of language, to language as nature," to the representational character of language that "appear[s] to be telling us something simple, literal, primitive: something *true*" (ibid.; emphasis in original). This is the "true" story that U.S. foreign-policy discourse attempts to tell. By having the first word— telling things as they "really"are and thereby structuring how stories get told—the United States attempts to guarantee its ability to have the last word as well. But systems of denotation and representation always end up telling us too much, always end up revealing themselves as mere representations that are certainly powerful stories but also simply myths because their meanings are generated as much from a system of connotation as they are from denotation. The connotative countercommunications generated by Castro's Cuba disrupt the conventional Cold War codes—the denotative structures—through which the U.S. story is told.

Taking my characters, scenes, and plot points from "Sarrasine," I turn to *S/Z* as a way to critically assess the telling of the story of U.S.–Cuban relations, a telling that tells a great deal about U.S.–Caribbean relations from the late 1950s onward. My story both reads and writes the story told by the United States concerning the Cuba of the late 1950s and early 1960s. As such, it rereads the story of U.S.–Cuban relations as yet another writerly text.

Like Herbert Matthews's *New York Times* story, my story unfolds as a drama in three parts. Yet it is less concerned with events in U.S.–Cuban relations than it is with characterizations, orientations, and sets. It examines the U.S.–Cuba story in terms of how the United

States characterized Cuba and itself, how Castro's Cuba resisted codification, and what effects the telling of this story has had on the United States and on U.S.–Caribbean relations more generally. My story, in other words, is a serialization about orientation, neut(e)ralization, and the contagion of castration.

Orientation

As the self-appointed designer of the modern Western Hemisphere, the United States approached vast territories of Latin America as a sculptor would a piece of clay, smoothing here, chiseling there to bring desired features into relief. Cuba was one such surface. U.S. policy molded Cuba as both a miniature of and a complement to the United States. As a miniature, Cuba was re-created in the image of American liberal democratic capitalism. Since the U.S. victory in the Spanish-American War of 1898 (a k a the Cuban War for Independence), which for a short time made Cuba a territory of the United States, the United States shaped Cuba militarily (by military rule from 1899 to 1902), politically (with the Cuban constitution simulating that of the United States), and economically (through a reciprocal economic treaty). "Batista's Cuba was a magnificent facade, a culmination of the nineteenth century ideal of a prosperous and happy land" (Langley, 1968: 168).

But there was another side to Cuba, that of U.S. complement. In this respect, Cuba appeared in the U.S. imaginary not just as a lesser, feminized copy of America but as iconically feminine. As such, Cuba was fully accessible to U.S. desires. During the Prohibition years, Cuba "became a national metaphor for romance, escapism, and sex," an image that was to linger in the American imaginary until the late 1950s (Black, 1988: 64). Consumed by Americans as "a forbidden, slightly overripe fruit" (ibid., 92), "Cuba was where respectable North Americans went to gamble without restraint, to see live sex shows of the most inventive character, to indulge without fear of discovery in whoring with partners of either sex, to drink and eat cheaply, to be waited on hand and foot" (Gosse, 1993: 46–47). In this Cuba, "ordinary US citizens took advantage of Batista's pimping of his own country" (ibid., 47).

Whether Cuba was positioned to reproduce U.S. hemispheric ideals (U.S. inseminations into Cuba flowered into miniature U.S. outposts in the Caribbean) or to affirm a U.S. masculine identity (the United States was a real man because it had a real woman at its beck and call), Cuba was always to be found in a feminine position vis-à-vis the United States. Protected by its protector, passive in the face of U.S. actions, dependent on an independent America—these were the dichotomous codes that oriented a U.S. reading of Cuba until 1959. It was this Cuba into which the United States read Fidel Castro.

> The Cuba into which Castro erupted in January 1959 had long appeared to accept Western political, social, and economic values. The existence in Cuban society... of collective blemishes and shortcomings was uncontested; the prevalent wisdom was that these would be mitigated or removed, when and if the national wealth increased, through the operation and the perfection of the methods of representative democracy. (U.S. ambassador to Cuba Philip Bonsal in 1959; Bonsal, 1971: 3).

Although Castro himself was viewed by some in the Eisenhower administration as a "collective blemish" on the Cuban body, the United States believed that Castro's imperfections would lessen in proportion to the increase in Cuban democratic institutions. Few, it seemed, were prepared for just how profoundly (and permanently?) Castro was transforming the Cuban body. President Eisenhower's inability to assess why Castro's Cuba might shun friendly U.S. advances in 1959 is a case in point:

> [H]ere is a country that you would believe, on the basis of our history, would be one of our real friends. The whole history—first of our intervention in 1898, our making and helping set up Cuban independence, ... the trade concessions we have made and the very close relationships that have existed most of the time with them—would seem to make it a puz-

zling matter to figure out just exactly why the Cubans and
the Cuban Government would be so unhappy when, after
all, their principal market is right here, their best market. I
don't know exactly what the difficulty is. (President's news
conference, October 28, 1959; Eisenhower, 1959: 271)

"The difficulty" in U.S.–Cuban relations that President Eisenhower could not identify is what Barbara Johnson calls the "critical
difference" Castro brings to Cuba. As Johnson explains, "Difference
is not engendered in the space between identities; it is what makes all
totalization of the identity of a self or the meaning of a text impossible" (B. Johnson, 1980: 4). The critical difference the hypermasculin-
ized Castro brought to the iconically feminized Cuba was a "difference within" Cuba itself. Such a difference "subverts the very idea of
identity, infinitely deferring the possibility of adding up the sum of a
text's parts or meanings and reaching a totalized, integrated whole"
(ibid.). Read in these terms, Cuba could never be solely iconically feminine nor hypermasculine. It would always be presented as a mixed,
untotalizable space.

Castro's critical difference affected the U.S. ability to read Cuba.
Wishing to find what it had found in a pre-Castro Cuba — a feminized depository for U.S. desires — the Eisenhower administration approached Cuba as a Barthesian readerly text, as an already completed
textual product. The Eisenhower administration identified in Cuba
"the already-read . . . that it must have in common with its reader in
order for it to be readable at all" (ibid., 3). The already-read in this
case was the series of dichotomous codes that enabled Cuba to be the
subservient supplement to U.S. hegemonic masculinity. It is not surprising, then, that the United States turned a blind eye to the critical
difference that Castro brought to Cuba because "[w]hen we read a
text once . . . we can see in it only what we have already learned to see
before" (ibid.). Failing to reread Castro's Cuba, the Eisenhower administration "was obliged to read the same story everywhere" (Barthes,
1974: 16), and in this story it read Cuba as it had learned to read her
before — as a feminine complement to U.S. masculinity.

But, at some juncture, as President Eisenhower's comments suggest, reading Castro's Cuba became a challenge, if not an impossibility. Castro transformed Cuba from a known body—a playground of pleasures—into an enigma, thereby frustrating the fulfillment of U.S. desires. No longer secure about its access to Castro's Cuba, the United States transformed its desire *for* Cuba (as complement/miniature) into a desire to *know* Cuba (what identity/sex is it?). In other words, knowledge about the Cuban body (its identity/sex) was to be gained prior to knowledge of the Cuban body (complement/miniature); and, because Cuba was already a known quantity in the U.S. imaginary (female), the United States focused its intelligence efforts on Castro.

The United States approached Castro's identity as a detective does a mystery. "Who was Castro, really?" was the question the Eisenhower administration asked. Privileging reading over writing and rereading, the United States persisted in viewing Castro's Cuba as a mystery. Eventually, the United States did make a decision about Castro's identity, for it was only by making Castro's "true" identity decidable that Castro's Cuba could be read. Couched in Cold War dichotomous codes, Castro was labeled a dictator, not a democrat, and a communist, not a capitalist. So described, he did not fit into the Western camp and necessarily (according to this bipolar logic) had to be in the Soviet camp.

But this move by the United States was a misreading, not because the United States placed Castro's Cuba on the wrong side of Cold War codes but because Castro's Cuba defied Cold War logics. By treating the undecidable as decidable, the United States refused to see the plurality of Cuba. As Barthes explains, "To choose, to decide on a hierarchy of codes, on a predetermination of messages . . . is *impertinent,* since it overwhelms the articulation of writing by a single voice . . . to miss the plurality of the codes is to censor the work of the discourse" (Barthes, 1974: 77; emphasis in original).

To appreciate what plural constitutes the text requires an interpretation of Castro's Cuba as a neuter. Neither marked by meaning nor unmarked by it, "the neuter is what comes *between* the mark and the non-mark." The space of the neuter is "the *supplement of classification,* it joins realms, passions, characters." In so doing, the neuter "is what *confuses* meaning, the norm, normality" (Barthes, 1976: 107; emphasis in original). In the case of U.S.–Cuban relations, it is what both constitutes Castro's Cuba and jams Cold War codes of meaning.

Neut(e)ralization

On the level of denotation, it is difficult not to think of Castro's Cuba as a neuter. In Spanish, "Castro" literally means "I castrate." Because a castrator requires an object, a denotative reading of Castro's name produces a castrating/castrated dichotomy that might structure U.S.–Cuban relations. Although initially on the active, castrating side of this dichotomy, Castro seemed to castrate the iconically feminine and therefore already symbolically castrated Cuba and later attempted to castrate the United States. Yet, in the act of castrating, Castro as castrator inevitably came in contact with the castrated (passive). According to Barthes, subjects engaged in relationships with the symbolically disempowered (castrated) end up losing their own power. Castration, according to Barthes, is contagious. In such a structure, Castro the castrator cannot escape becoming Castro the castrated.

This denotatively derived structuring device can explain many aspects of U.S.–Cuban relations and should not be discarded. However, this device is itself enmeshed in a system of dichotomous representations. There are two key positions in the story it is able to tell (active versus passive, empowered versus disempowered), and the story itself is about repositionings that take place on the castrating/castrated dichotomy. What this dichotomy (and denotation in general) neglects are those aspects of a text that elude and disrupt representation. This "noise" or "static" that cannot be represented appears in a text, but it does so differently, as nonpositions, nondefinitions, or nonbeings. The noise that "corrupts the purity of communication" Barthes defines as connotation (Barthes, 1974: 9). To interpret the plural that constructs the text, then, one must move from denotation to connotation.

Connotatively, Castro's Cuba is a mixed figure. It is where Castro's hypermasculinity meets but is not blended with Cuba's iconic femininity. As they are conjoined in Castro's Cuba, neither femininity nor masculinity alone marks this political space. Rather, both genders saturate this space, transforming it from a space dominated by one gender or another into a medley of differences (Serres, 1987: 85). As such, Castro's Cuba is what Barthes calls the "and/or"—a symbol of nondecidability (Barthes, 1974: 77). It is similar to a hermaphrodite space that is characterized by the inclusion of various gender characteristics without the dominance of any one of them (Serres, 1987: 85). All that is excluded in this space is exclusion itself. As Michel Serres notes, eradicating the dominant, the law of the father (phallic law), is the most profound meaning of castration (ibid., 81–82).

Grafting Castro onto Cuba symbolically transforms Cuba from feminine to castrato. This is not a simple reversal of the masculine versus feminine and active versus passive dichotomies but the creation of an axis of undecidability that makes sexual (and other) distinctions impossible. As Barthes reminds us, the castrato "is the blind and mobile flaw in this system [of representation]; he moves back and forth between active and passive: castrated, he castrates"(Barthes, 1974: 36).

Castro's Cuba, positioned as castrato, neuter, hermaphrodite, is undecipherable. No hermeneutic code will ever succeed in uncovering the "truth" it conceals because, if there is a secret about Castro's Cuba, it is that there is literally "nothing" to be deciphered. Beyond and behind realist codes of representation, there is "nothing"but surface and appearance. There is no "known" form.

The Cold War might be described as *"the history of the ordering of noise in codes"* according to the dominant antitheses of the times— capitalist versus communist, democrat versus dictator, West versus East, and so on (Attali, 1985: 5; emphasis in original). "[T]he antithesis is the battle between two plenitudes set ritually face to face like two fully armed warriors; the Antithesis is the figure of the *given* opposition, eternal, eternally recurrent: the figure of the inexpiable" (Barthes, 1974: 27; emphasis in original). As such, it cannot tolerate that which it cannot identify and classify. What this code demands is that all subjects and activities be named, and, once named, be positioned on one side of the antithesis or the other.

During the Cold War, Castro's Cuba (like any other neuter) was necessarily excluded. For the Soviets, Cuba's exclusion was at first a matter of geopolitics, for Cuba was located in a forbidden hemisphere. For the United States, Cuba had been excluded since 1898 but in a different form. First as a military protectorate, then as a geopoliticial space guarded (via the Platt Amendment) and partially occupied (Guantánamo Bay Naval Base) by the United States, Cuba already was a form of nonbeing; for Cuba was not a fully sovereign space. These aspects of nonbeing were precisely what drew the United States toward Cuba. So long as Cuba remained dependent on the United States, Cuba's political exclusion (nonsovereign being) did not threaten U.S. self-understandings. Cuba was a second-order copy of an idealized U.S. self-image. All that was demanded of it was that it remain accessible to U.S. desires.

Once Castro was grafted onto Cuba, a new political form was generated, and this form was the revolutionary state. Like a neuter, this form of political nonidentity was regarded as unnatural. As Castro himself once commented, "Nobody is born a revolutionary. A revolutionary is formed through a process" (Castro to Lee Lockwood in 1965; quoted in Domingues, 1989: 31). Located neither on the active nor passive, West nor East, capitalist nor communist side of Cold War dichotomies, Castro's revolutionary Cuba—like Castro himself—is reversible. As Castro put it, "Everything's reversible. I'm reversible" (quoted in Geyer, 1993: 371). Located in a nonposition, Castro's Cuba could pass freely from one side of a dichotomy to another. In so doing, it jammed Cold War codes that, grounded in bipolar logics, demanded irreversibility. Like the nonaligned movement it led, Castro's Cuba was fatal to Cold War codes because it actively removed the divide between the terms West and East (Barthes, 1974: 215–16).

The Contagion of Castration

The mixed figure of Castro's Cuba is the "blind and mobile flaw in the system" of Cold War codes that "moves back and forth between active and passive" — between East and West — engendering misreadings of its neut(e)rality and determinations on behalf of both superpowers to incorporate it into their own blocs/bodies (ibid., 36). What the superpowers did not count on was that these incorporations would spread the contagion of castration to each of them, albeit in vastly different ways. Soviet premier Nikita Khrushchev, for example, was granted "early retirement" by the Central Committee because of the humiliation suffered by the Soviets in the 1962 Cuban missile crisis. The symbolic castration of the United States occurred a year earlier. As a result of the failed Bay of Pigs invasion, President Kennedy was to lose "face" (phallic/hegemonic power) within and beyond the United States, a loss he and his country believed they had recovered from with America's tough stand in the Cuban missile crisis but that was an irreplaceable loss. Some have even suggested that Kennedy's loss of face in the Bay of Pigs was the root cause of his literally losing his head in 1963. As one commentator put it, "President Kennedy, massively bruised by the [Bay of Pigs] debacle, . . . moved toward decisions — regarding the CIA, Cuba, Vietnam, the Soviet Union — which, in some analyses, were to determine his own assassination" (Simons, 1996: 297).

Whatever the speculation, the "real" and "imaginary" causes and consequences of the U.S. invasion of the Bay of Pigs and the Cuban missile crisis can never be sorted out. They stand out in U.S. foreign-policy discourse, if not in the U.S. imaginary, as a tragedy and a triumph in which "reality" and "myth" — "denotation" and "connotation" — are strikingly mixed but not quite blended. As such, these two events epitomize both the "actual" and the "symbolic" contagion of castration in the triangulated relations between the Soviet Union, the United States, and Cuba in the early 1960s. It is not surprising, then, that they correspond well to scenes from Balzac's story "Sarrasine."

The Bay of Pigs illustrates the U.S. desire to misread the neuter as a woman and to possess "her" by kidnapping Cuba from Castro, a scene that parallels Sarrasine's more successful kidnapping of La Zambinella but that for both the United States and Sarrasine contaminated them with castration. The Cuban missile crisis reveals the frustration of the United States at its inability to carry out its vengeance against Castro's Cuba both because the United States was symbolically castrated by the Bay of Pigs invasion and because it cannot castrate the already castrated. The United States comes to terms with this by giving up on its desire to have Cuba, all the while ensuring that no one else may have "her" either. The drama of the Cuban missile crisis maps well onto Sarrasine's tormented attack on La Zambinella. Unable either to have La Zambinella or to kill "her," Sarrasine accepts his own symbolic castration through inviting his death by "falling" on the sword of La Zambinella's protector.

Kidnappings and Contagions

Attempted kidnappings of Castro's Cuba by the United States have never been (straight)forward. Although the United States first hoped to retain and later to restore Castro's Cuba within the Western bloc as a feminine figure that would secure a U.S. foothold in the Caribbean, it was a matter of speculation as to how this was to be achieved. Should Castro's Cuba be kidnapped as a composite figure? If so, this implies that Castro was a force not to be feared by the United States but, like Cuba before him, one to be molded into a useful figure for the United States. The early wooing of Castro by the Eisenhower administration suggests that it was precisely this strategy that the United States initially pursued. Even in the face of much evidence that Castro could not be wooed, the United States persisted in this position long after any hope of success had passed; for whenever the United States looked to Cuba — even Castro's Cuba — it wished to read and therefore did read Cuba as it had read her before: as a feminine complement to U.S. masculinity. Failing to reread Cuba or to view Cuba as a writerly text — as a text always under production — the United States simply proceeded to read the already read in Cuba, thus viewing Castro as a blotch or a "blemish" but not as a permanent impediment to its happy relationship with a repossessed, feminized Cuba.

But in July 1960, the Soviets made a play for Cuba that initiated a change in U.S. foreign policy. Khrushchev publicly criticized U.S. economic moves against Cuba — moves designed to pressure Castro to get back into line with "hemispheric" interests (Weldes and Saco, 1996: 374–75). Khrushchev interpreted these moves as possibly "the beginning of preparations for intervention against Cuba." Such activities by the United States would not be tolerated by the Soviet Union. Khrushchev announced that "we for our part shall do everything to support Cuba and its courageous people in the struggle for the freedom and national independence they have won under the leadership of their national leader, Fidel Castro." Nor should the United States feel it had a free hand in the hemisphere because of its close proximity to Cuba and the great distance between the Soviet Union and the Western Hemisphere. Khrushchev warned the United States, "It should not be forgotten that the United States is not so inaccessibly distant from the Soviet Union as it used to be." And then he offered Castro's Cuba a figurative/figural cover to supplement its neut(e)ral status — an artificial phallus in the form of rockets launched from the Soviet Union. "*Figuratively* speaking, in case of need Soviet artillerymen can support the Cuban people with their rocket fire if the aggressive forces in the Pentagon dare to launch an intervention against Cuba" (*FRUS, 1958–1960*, 6: 996; my emphasis). In this form, the Soviets championed themselves as Cuba's protector.

The Soviet move offered President Eisenhower an opportunity to disown the increasingly embarrassing Castro's Cuba without having to concede Cold War codes. The president proclaimed that Khrushchev's announcement "underscores the close ties that have developed between the Soviet and Cuban Governments. It also shows the clear intention to establish Cuba in a role serving Soviet purposes in this hemisphere" (ibid.). Ceasing to be a trophy mistress of the United States, Castro's Cuba now served to perversely prop up Soviet masculinity in a region forbidden to it. The president continued, "I affirm in the most emphatic terms that the United States will not be deterred from its responsibilities by the threats Mr. Khrushchev is making. Nor will the United States . . . permit the establishment of a regime dominated by international communism in the Western Hemisphere" (ibid., 997).

Even in light of President Eisenhower's remarks, not everyone in the United States was ready to accept that Castro or Castro's Cuba was lost to the Soviets. When Vice President Nixon met with Castro in 1959, Nixon wrote of Castro, "He is either incredibly naive about Communism or under Communist discipline — my guess is the former" (ibid., 476). Might Castro still be "incredibly naive about Communism"? Reports of Castro's initial reactions to the Soviet offer of missiles encouraged this view. Days after Khrushchev's speech, the U.S. ambassador to Cuba cabled Washington that "Fidel Castro was caught entirely off base by Khrushchev's July 9 statement about what Russia would do to us if we invaded Cuba. The rumor, as I get it, is that he was perfectly furious about a development which puts Cuba entirely under the Soviet wing" (ibid., 1008–9). Discussions among members of the National Security Council (NSC) echoed this sentiment. National Security Adviser Allen Dulles received information that Castro was having "second thoughts" about "the 'hug of the bear'" and had stated that "Cuba does not depend for the preservation of its independence on Soviet rockets" (ibid., 1014). Cuba's independence — its neut(e)rality — depended instead on its lack of "rockets."

These discussions resulted in a short-lived belief in U.S. security circles that Castro was not a communist but rather was under communist control. "It was probable," they concluded, "that Castro was no longer his own master" (ibid., 1039). Castro appeared to some to be a Soviet prisoner, pinned down by this aggressive Soviet pledge of protection. It was the naive yet manly Castro whom the Soviets seemed to desire more than the iconically feminine Cuba, an image that fit well with U.S. images of a perverted Soviet state. This was a time for U.S. heroism. Castro needed to be kidnapped from the Soviets before they penetrated both him and the hemisphere. Otherwise, it was anyone's guess as to whether or not the United States would ever be in a position to reclaim Cuba. U.S. officials contemplated offering Castro the assurances of "asylum in the event he found himself in danger. Perhaps we could fly Castro out of Cuba and get him on our side" (ibid.).

These heroic queries by U.S. officials illustrate an interesting moment in the reengendering of the U.S. relationship with Castro's Cuba. Determined to preserve its image of Cuba as iconically feminine, the United States took to reading Castro as a heroic albeit inexperienced masculine figure who needed a helping hand from the United States if he were to protect his country from the grips of Soviet-style Communism. But a heroic rescue by the United States of the heroically figured Castro has no place in masculine/feminine, active/passive dichotomies. There is something very queer here. Not surprisingly, even though the United States recognized a queer component in the Soviet–Cuban relationship, it failed to read this element into its own relationship with Castro's Cuba—a failure it would count on through the next three decades in its increasingly queer quest to compensate for its symbolic castration at the hands of Castro's Cuba.

U.S. hopes of rescuing Castro from "international Communism" and receiving not just Cuba as its reward for hemispheric valor but Castro's Cuba were short-lived. By late September 1960, "Mr. Dulles believed that under the Castro regime, Cuba was now virtually a member of the Communist Bloc" (ibid., 1074). A dispatch from the U.S. embassy in Cuba in early November said, "The Castro regime is now believed to be so firmly committed to the communist camp that it could not extract itself even in the unlikely event that it might wish to do so" (ibid., 1125). The kidnapping would have to be rethought. What was now called for was a U.S. kidnapping not of Castro from

Communism but of Cuba from Castro. This was the officially stated purpose of U.S. involvement in the invasion of the Bay of Pigs. "Our objection isn't to the Cuban Revolution," the Kennedy administration stressed. "[I]t is to the fact that Castro has turned it over to the Communists" (Schlesinger, 1965: 222). Thus, the Kennedy administration embarked on "the least covert military operation in history," an operation that the press had long been reporting about as if it were "a kidnapping—not a military operation whose entire success might depend on the elements of surprise and secrecy" (Salinger, 1966: 147, 146).

If, as Jacques Lacan suggests, the phallus only functions when it is veiled and therefore phallic power coded as hegemonic power is only successful when it is invisible, the Bay of Pigs invasion might best be described as an active loss of cover for the United States: just before the invasion, Castro imprisoned any subversive, "undercover" elements he knew of in the country; during the invasion, Kennedy refused to cover the repatriated Cuban exiles on the ground with the planned number of air strikes or other overt assistance by the United States; and after the invasion, the Kennedy administration and the United States suffered from a domestic, regional, and global loss of face (phallic cover). U.S. credibility and U.S. hegemony were never so actively doubted during the Cold War as they were in the aftermath of this invasion.

Although President Kennedy promised that the United States would continue to "show its will" against communism to protect smaller states in the Americas, even he recognized that this exposure was not necessarily the right strategy. Armies and nuclear armaments— the primary elements of the U.S. security "shield"—were not enough to combat communism because "subversion, infiltration, and a host of other tactics steadily advance, picking off vulnerable areas one by one in situations which do not permit our own armed intervention. . . . [O]ur security," Kennedy now recognized, "may be lost piece by piece" (Kennedy, 1961: 306). And so could U.S. hegemony. As a result of the Bay of Pigs invasion, the United States lost a piece of itself. It found itself without its Cuban mistress and in doubt of its mastery over Latin American and global affairs. It was a symbolically castrated, headless hegemon in search of something it did not have but desperately wished to believe it (still?) possessed—the phallus.

The Cuban missile crisis that occurred the next year is (un)conventionally read as the moment of rephallusization of the Kennedy administration and the United States more generally. President Kennedy's hard-line insistence that the Soviets stop building bases in Cuba as well as dismantle and return the so-called offensive weapons in Cuba to the Soviet Union under United Nations verification seemingly produced the very results that the United States hoped for in the hemisphere. Beyond simply achieving the denotative content of its directive, the United States also achieved connotative capital. For example, the contagion of castration spread to Premier Khrushchev, who was forced from power, but the contagion did not (yet) spread to the small states of Latin America that the United States had vowed to protect. Additionally, the United States claimed credit for preventing the phallusization of Castro's Cuba. Although the neutered Cuba rhetorically recemented its symbolic alignment with the Soviet Union, it did not retain the figurative phallus the Soviets had offered it in the form of nuclear missiles on its territory.

But the outcome the United States most hoped for was not to be. The United States was not itself rephallusized by the Cuban missile crisis. Even though it prevented what it viewed as a militaristic Soviet expansion into Cuba from transforming the Caribbean Sea/See into a Communist lake, Cuba was not returned to the United States as the feminine complement who mirrored back U.S. masculinity intact. The best the Caribbean Sea/See could now do was to reflect back U.S. identity in pieces—"piece by piece"—for the Sea/See itself was now divided into Cuban and non-Cuban pieces. If the United States was able to see its hegemonic masculinity reflected back to itself in the Caribbean Sea/See at all since Castro's assumption of power, it saw itself with a phallus that was detachable. The U.S. body was now a body in pieces. The U.S. "post-phallic" era had begun.

Neither the Kennedy administration nor subsequent U.S. administrations ever forgave Castro's Cuba for America's de(tachable)phallusization. Immediately after the Cuban missile crisis, covert activities against Castro's Cuba were renewed with a vengeance in the form of Operation Mongoose. While previously designed to assassinate Castro and his masculine character (by plotting to have his beard fall out, for example), this operation was now targeted at Cuba "her"self (Walker, 1994: 58). So, too, continued the U.S. economic embargo against Cuba, an embargo that—with the 1996 passage of the Helms-Burton bill—put America's sculpturesque skills to another use; for this bill "chiselled in stone" "Washington's 35-year[-]old hostility" toward Cuba (Leogrande, 1997: 211). The United States, in a sense, acted and continues to act as the stereotypical jealous-turned-brutal spurned spouse. If the United States could not have Cuba, she must die. Then no one could have her. No one could take her away from the United States or remind the United States that it had lost her and, in losing Cuba, had lost its phallic identity.

But the United States failed even at this. Like La Zambinella for Sarrasine, Castro's Cuba for the United States was neither male nor female. It was both. As such, it was beyond nature and therefore beyond death. Located beyond Cold War codes, Castro's Cuba continued to corrupt the purity of communication of global affairs. This is the remaining consequence of the Cuban missile crisis that is often overlooked. However rhetorically realigned Castro's Cuba became with the Soviet Union after this episode, paradoxically the Cuban missile crisis released Castro's Cuba from "the hug of the bear" that had begun to embrace it in July 1960. The Cuban–Soviet relationship was quite turbulent during the 1960s, and improved during the 1970s and 1980s only to rupture under Mikhail Gorbachev. Castro's Cuba, the Cuban missile crisis proved, could never be fully aligned with either superpower. It continued to play the role of the "blind and mobile flaw" in the Cold War system that neither superpower could fully retain or relinquish. As a body beyond sex and of questionable gender, Castro's Cuba continues to disrupt the U.S. imaginary image of its hegemonic identity by queering the content of its masculinity; for Castro's reign reminds the United States that what it desires in Cuba cannot be just the iconic femininity of Cuba, because the United States wooed Cuba long after Castro came to power.

Love and Loss in the Cycle of Castration

If contact with a neuter draws one into the cycle of castration, why pursue/woo a neuter in the first place? The answer, according to Barbara Johnson, has to do with narcissistic love:

> Upon seeing La Zambinella for the first time, Sarrasine exclaims: "To be loved by her, or to die!" This alternative places all of the energy of the passion not on the object, La Zambinella, but on the subject, Sarrasine. To be loved, or to die; to exist as the desired object, or not to exist at all. What is at stake is not the union between two people, but the narcissistic awakening of one. Seeing La Zambinella is Sarrasine's first experience of *himself* as an object of love. By means of the image of sculpturesque perfection, Sarrasine thus falls in love with none other than himself. (B. Johnson, 1980: 9)

The same can be said of the relationship between the United States and Cuba. What puzzles President Eisenhower in 1959 is Cuba's rejection of the United States as its desired object: "[H]ere is a country that you would believe, on the basis of our history, would be one of our real friends.... You would think they would want good relationships" (Eisenhower, 1959: 271). What is doubly curious for President Eisenhower is that, in the U.S. view, the United States has long been Cuba's desired object—its ideal political, cultural, and economic partner. Since its "rescue" of the feminized Cuba, the United States had relied on Cuba to reflect its narcissistic image back to it in the form of hegemonic masculinity. Yet, although the United States persisted in believing that Cuba viewed it as its ideal partner even after Castro came on the scene, the United States was incapable of being an ideal partner to anyone but itself. Like Narcissus, the United States was not seeking an ideal partner in another. It was in love with an ideal image of itself. "Losing Cuba" might force the United States to confront its narcissistic desires and what these desires might reveal.

It is therefore not surprising that, like Sarrasine, first President Eisenhower and later President Kennedy were willingly led through a series of delusions: Cuba as U.S. protectorate, Castro as emerging democrat, Castro as Soviet prisoner, and so on. It is only after Cuba ceased to function as the inverted mirror of U.S. potency that the United States acted to avenge its honor and to restore itself as a loved object — by kidnapping (Bay of Pigs) and by challenging the castrato's protector (Cuban missile crisis).

Both moves were destined to fail, however, because U.S. desires were misplaced. What the United States desired was to rid the Caribbean of the critical difference that Castro's Cuba brings to the region. But in so doing, the United States persisted in seeing this not as a difference within Castro's Cuba, but a difference between — first between Cuba and Castro and later between the East and the West. Yet, because difference is located within Castro's Cuba, it cannot be eradicated; it can only be spread. Whenever the United States attempts to dispel or displace this difference so that it can restore Cuba as the feminized mirror that will mirror back U.S. masculinity, the United States is confronted with cracks within this mirror that expose the U.S. body as a body in pieces — as a symbolically castrated body that can thereafter never be mirrored back whole. This is consistent with how Barbara Johnson describes castration: "as the literalization of the difference within which prevents any subject from coinciding with itself" (B. Johnson, 1980: 10). As with Sarrasine, the big mistake the United States made was in thinking it knew where difference was located — between subjects (sexes, poles), not within the self (Castro's Cuba, United States). Having incorporated its own difference/symbolic castration within itself through its contact with Castro's Cuba, the American body politic ceases to coincide with its longed-for imaginary image of itself — as straight, as masculine, as phallic, as hegemonic, as whole.

The tragedy for the United States is that it misread the symbolic, connotative content of castration, both for Castro's Cuba and for itself. Compelled by its narcissistic drive to be the loved object for Cuba, the United States through its courting of Castro's Cuba symbolically courted its own castration. Like Sarrasine, the United States was unable to love the other for itself, no matter its sex or sexual combination (ibid.).

What, then, is the role of the neuter, of Castro's Cuba? Once grafted onto Cuba, Castro articulates/performs that which must not be named — castration. "[L]ike the writerly, castration is a process of production, an active and violent indetermination" (ibid., 8). Castration is that "which subverts the very foundation of any affirmation of value. Castration can neither be assumed nor denied, but only enacted in the return of unsuitable difference in every text" (ibid., 12). Both in name (I castrate) and activity (I cannot be aligned), Castro rewrites the writerly text of Cuba and reveals a "truth" to the United States that proves to be fatal to its sense of hegemonic masculinity. To paraphrase Barbara Johnson, Castro's Cuba destroys the United States' "reassuring masculinity by revealing that it is based on castration. But [the U.S.] realization that he himself is thereby castrated, that he is looking at his true mirror image [in Castro's Cuba or in a fragmented Caribbean Sea/See], is still blind to the fact that he had never been capable of loving in the first place. His love was from the beginning the cancellation and castration of the other" (ibid., 10). What better description is there of the exercise of hegemonic power!

As with Sarrasine, what proves to be fatal to the U.S. image of itself is its failure to reread Castro's Cuba, to appreciate Castro's Cuba as another writerly text. At the end of Balzac's story, Sarrasine recognizes his mistake, accepts his castration, and invites his own death as penance for confounding the codes of nature. At the end of my story in this chapter, the United States makes no such sacrifice. Refusing to reread Castro's Cuba as a strategic refusal to reread itself, the United States makes Castro's Cuba bear the burden of its failed seduction by the United States. Only in this way can the sacred story the United

States tells itself be preserved and the U.S. confrontation with its own symbolic castration be deferred. For the next thirty years, the United States desperately diverts its eyes (which is easy to do because it lost its head over Cuba) from the images of itself it might find in the fatally fractured Caribbean Sea/See—as post-phallic, posthegemonic, and positively queer. And its narcissistic tale continues, next to be enacted in the Dominican Republic.

3. America's Primary Colors in the Dominican Republic

American preoccupations in the Caribbean culminated in the 1965 U.S. invasion of the Dominican Republic. Using poetic turned geographic license, a contemporary cartoon shows three landmasses protruding from the Caribbean Sea—in the foreground the island of Cuba, behind Cuba the island of Hispaniola on which the Dominican Republic is located, and in the background what might be the geographically misplaced but symbolically well-placed Florida peninsula (for, although the United States is geographically closer to Cuba, in 1965 it was symbolically closer to the Dominican Republic—economically, politically, and ideologically). Turbulent forces have been unleashed over the Caribbean, forces that the cartoon suggests possibly penetrate geopolitical boundaries. They appear as a swarm of needle-nosed bloodsucking mosquitoes hovering above and venturing beyond Cuba into other Latin locations. The cartoon labels Cuba as "infested" and marks it as a breeding ground of the "red threat." But this pestilence does not go unchecked. Uncle Sam is pictured taking a firm stand against the communist menace, a stand expressed both by his feet firmly planted on imaginary American soil and by the exceedingly large fumigation gun he holds waist high in front of him. From his cleansing cannon he sprays a deadly poison at the communist contagion, killing the mosquito that threatened the Dominican Republic. Rephallusized, ready for action, and indeed in action, the United States appears in this cartoon as if it has recovered from its confrontation with Castro's Cuba.

Yet the cartoon's caption introduces a troubling doubt into this interpretation. It reads: "Why not get the breeding ground?" thereby suggesting that the United States has inappropriately aimed its fatal phallus. Or—even more troubling—the cartoon gives the impression that the United States may not have a working phallus at all, for, if it possessed the potency to extinguish the contagious Cuba, it would surely use it to sterilize this red menace and sanitize the region. The exaggerated display of phallic power in the United States' 1965 invasion of the Dominican Republic denies the "fact" that the United States was symbolically castrated by Castro's Cuba, thereby effectively exposing U.S. impotency in the region all the more, symbolized in this cartoon by Uncle Sam's formidable yet faulty fumigation device.

If Castro's Cuba and the Caribbean Sea/See generally confront the United States with its primary narcissism—its "tendency to treat others as a mirror of the self" (Lasch, 1991: 239)—then the Dominican Republic confronts the United States with its secondary narcissism: its attempt "to annul the pain of disappointed love" that it experienced in its loss of Cuba (ibid., 240). The United States is determined to have a feminized, noncommunist Dominican Republic as a securing substitute for the womanly Cuba who betrayed it for communist Castro.

Yet, in its confrontation with Castro's Cuba, the United States lost something more precious than Cuba: its unquestionable hegemonic masculinity and the phallic power that accompanies it. But this is a loss that the United States necessarily fails to recognize. As in the case of Castro's Cuba, the United States fails to reread itself, once again denying the writerly content of the Caribbean. In this sense, U.S. involvement in the Dominican Republic is consistent with Sigmund Freud's characterization of melancholia. As Freud explains, the melancholic "knows *whom* he has lost but not *what* he has lost in him" (Freud, 1984: 254). Reflecting on its loss of Cuba, the United States deflects from its gaze the traumatic evidence that would reveal to it

what it has lost in losing Cuba. At the intersection of the differently designed mirrors of Cuba and the Dominican Republic lies a panorama
of problems for U.S. policymakers that play themselves out in patri-
otic technicolor.

Prismatic Preoccupations

> Women have served all these centuries as looking-glasses, pos-
> sessing the magic and delicious power of reflecting the figure
> of a man at twice its natural size.
>
> — *Virginia Woolf*

The Caribbean Sea/See is awash with mirrors for the United States.
There is the Caribbean Sea itself, a fluid, feminized form into which
the United States traditionally looks to find its masculine, hegemonic
identity reflected back to it at no less than "twice its natural size."
But the U.S. encounter with Castro's Cuba fractured both the Caribbean Sea/See and the U.S. fantasy that it could forever serenely specu-
late its hegemonic manhood in this specular space. And, in the early
1960s, the Dominican Republic found itself located in the U.S. imaginary at an acute angle from the communist would-be conqueror.

The result was a prismatic effect. In what had been the "colorless"/white-dominated feminine space of the Caribbean now lurked a
cacophony of color — brown-skinned otherness, red-blooded communism, and the faintest shade of lascivious lavender. As in a well-crafted
cartoon, each of these colors marks both a caricature (of the Hapless
Hispanic, the Contagious Castro, and the Queer Compensator) and
an emotion-laden twin (domination, disease, denial). Not wanting to
turn its sights toward Cuba — the poisonous palette from which these
colors spilled onto and into the Caribbean mirror turned prism — in
the 1960s the United States determinately set its sights on the Dominican Republic, as a second-best Caribbean concubine, as a "showcase
for democracy," as an embodiment of U.S. virility.

This was not the first time that the United States contorted its
concentration toward the Dominican Republic. Indeed, the Domini-

can Republic has long been a location of "international importance out of proportion to its size, population, and resources" because of the "high level of visibility" it has received in its relations with the United States (Wiarda and Kryzanek, 1982: 133). Historically, this visibility has meant that foiled U.S. attempts to purchase the Dominican Republic in the 1800s were followed in the next century by U.S. military occupations and economic agreements (such as U.S. direct control of Dominican customs) that made a mockery of the political and economic sovereignty of this Caribbean state.

Symbolically, this visibility means that the Dominican Republic often functions as a mirror for the United States that—unlike Cuba—does not reflect back U.S. hegemonic identity directly but rather reflects it in relation to some other place and/or time. Unlike the reflective surface that was Cuba, the Dominican Republic functions in the U.S. imaginary as a refractive surface. As such, it deflects light/knowledge/images at a certain symbolic angle, because these images always enter into the Dominican Republic obliquely from another medium of different density—Cuba, the United States, and so on. Already laden with the immense meaning of its connection to the Caribbean Sea/See—in which the Dominican Republic was viewed by the United States as a sanitized sanctuary where U.S. manly desires could be asserted and satisfied—the Dominican Republic had its meaning deflected into yet another space in the 1960s, the differently dense Vietnam.

The Dominican Republic was dubbed by one scholar "Vietnam writ small" (Wiarda, 1975: 835). Like Vietnam, the Dominican Republic was a place where the United States "went blithely on, swept up with the kind of reformist, Peace Corps mood of the time, not questioning the assumptions on which its policy was built, myopically seeking to transfer American solutions and modes of thinking and an American developmental model to a nation and society where they did not fit." U.S. policy in the Dominican Republic tells "much the same story and carr[ies] many of the same lessons as emerged from the 'Pentagon Papers' on Vietnam—that is, the incredible myopia and ethnocentrism that pervades American foreign policy, the tendency to manipulate and interfere" (ibid.).

It was not just within its sweeping economic/development agenda that U.S. actions in the Dominican Republic resembled those in Vietnam. The parallel continued in the way President Lyndon Johnson made his military decisions there. Another scholar noted of the Dominican invasion:

> It was, in a way, Vietnam all over again; as at Pleiku, he [President Johnson] did what he thought to be the bare minimum. At the outset in the Dominican Republic, he strove to hold open the option to whatever else might be judged necessary. As in Vietnam, he switched from one purpose to another almost imperceptibly: in Vietnam, from reprisal raids to systematic bombing; in the Dominican Republic, from a mercy mission to a rebellion-blocking mission. (Geyelin, 1966: 254)

The Dominican Republic, then, was a miniature mirror turned symbolically productive prism. The same egocentric and escalating tendencies that the United States demonstrated in Southeast Asia seemed in this Latin location to find their prismatic parallel, however microscopic and even modest they seemed in comparison. But miniature does not mean minor. Indeed, Secretary of State Dean Rusk believed that occurrences in the Dominican Republic provided the United States with "another test of U.S. resolve, whether it was something deliberately planned in Moscow or something which materialized spontaneously, but which the Communists could inevitably be expected to exploit. If the United States failed the test, its hand would, by this reasoning, be weaker in Vietnam" (ibid.). The United States had little choice but to take big action, for, as Walter Lippmann wrote of the Dominican intervention, "It is normal, not abnormal, for a great power to insist that within its sphere of influence no other great power [such as the Soviet Union via its Cuban satellite] shall exercise hostile military and political force" (quoted in Heren, 1970: 96).

Therefore, the minute became magnified in 1965. Although it at first mimicked U.S. policy toward Vietnam with its indecisiveness—

to the point that one commentator labeled it a "confuse-in" (see Lowenthau, 1972: 5)—the U.S. intervention in the Dominican Republic soon promised to be the kind of clean, quick military success the United States longed for in Vietnam. This was a display of U.S. will and power. There would be "no second Cuba" in the Dominican Republic, the Johnson administration declared. Moreover, unlike in Vietnam, the United States was in a position to enforce its words. If, in the wake of the U.S. loss of the Vietnam War, American popular cultural images such as the Rambo films asked, "Do we get to win this time?" the U.S. invasion of the Dominican Republic decisively and more immediately answered, "Yes, this time we get to beat the communists."

President Johnson—looking into the Dominican prism—saw America's primary colors (red, white, and blue) reflected and refracted. He told the American people, "where American citizens go that flag goes with them to protect them." Nostalgically, he continued:

> As a little boy I learned a declamation that I had to say in grade school. I don't remember all of it but a little of it is appropriate here this afternoon. It went something like this: "I have seen the glory of art and architecture. I have seen the sun rise on Mont Blanc. But the most beautiful vision that these eyes ever beheld was the flag of my country in a foreign land." (L. B. Johnson, 1966: 480)

It is through the colors of "Old Glory" that the 1965 U.S. invasion of the Dominican Republic unfurls.

Seeing Red

The loss of Cuba reddened the United States with embarrassment. What did it mean for U.S. hemispheric hegemony that the United States was forced to tolerate a Soviet satellite state ninety miles from its border? "Here [in Latin America] was half of the western hemisphere, which, if it turned against the United States, would mock our [U.S.] leadership before the world and create a hard and lasting threat to our national security" (Schlesinger, 1965: 177). With this in mind, blushing soon turned to brandishing as the United States under the Kennedy administration read the Caribbean context through its readerly concerns with Castro's Cuba and announced its "no second Cuba" policy. Under President Kennedy, the United States would "prevent any new state from going down the Castro road and so giving the Soviet Union a second bridgehead in the hemisphere" (ibid., 772). But the poisonous palette of Cuba seemed to be seeping into the Caribbean Sea/See, and everywhere the United States looked it saw red. It was feared that "Cuba had become 'an action base from which teams of communists, backed by the Soviet Union and Communist China, are seeking to turn the Caribbean Sea into a Communist lake'" (*New York Times,* January 4, 1961: 6; quoted in Weldes and Saco, 1996: 381).

Containing Caribbean losses to the communists took on even greater importance when Dominican dictator General Rafael Trujillo was assassinated in May 1961. Fearing that Trujillo's repressive regime—like Batista's pre-Castro regime in Cuba—would produce another revolutionary movement led by a Castro-type figure, the United States had backed all manner of covert, "preemptive" attempts to remove Trujillo from power since 1959 (Rabe, 1988: 153–62). Faced with "success," President Kennedy's response to this news was to outline U.S. policy options in the Dominican Republic. "There are three possibilities in descending order of preference: a decent democratic regime, a continuation of the Trujillo regime, or a Castro regime. We ought to aim at the first, but we really can't renounce the second until we are sure that we can avoid the third" (Schlesinger, 1965: 704–5).

Trying to "avoid the third" (communist) option was part of the impetus for the Kennedy administration's "Alliance for Progress" program, a sort of good-neighbor policy revived in a presumably collective, collaborative form involving the United States with Latin America. The Kennedy administration reasoned that "if the United States were not ready to offer an affirmative program for democratic modernization [in Latin America], new Castros would undoubtedly rise across the continent" (ibid., 177). With the election of Juan Bosch as president of the newly democratic Dominican Republic in December

1962 and his embracing of the Alliance, the Kennedy administration saw in this island state a possible "democratic showcase in the Caribbean" (ibid., 708).

But in the Johnson administration's view, Bosch did not prove to be much of a leader. Having alienated both the right and the left, he was overthrown in September 1963. The U.S. government under President Lyndon Johnson allowed a series of military and military-backed civilian governments to replace Bosch. When "revolution" broke out on April 24, 1965, in the name of restoring President Bosch to power, the United States, having lost all faith in Bosch's ability to govern, withheld support for the rebel forces.

Yet, however much the United States had waffled in its support of Bosch, it was not prepared to go into the red again by losing another Caribbean state to communism. Red this time with passion, President Johnson sent in the U.S. Marines on April 28, 1965. In the following days, Johnson offered a series of justifications for the U.S. intervention, each of them increasingly flushed with red-inspired rhetoric intent on repulsing the crimson communists.

On April 28, Johnson told the American public, "I have ordered the Secretary of Defense to put the necessary American troops ashore in order to give protection to hundreds of Americans who are still in the Dominican Republic and to escort them safely back to this country" (L. B. Johnson, 1966: 461). Two days later, he repeated his original justification and embellished it with the assurance that "We took this step when, and only when, we were officially notified by police and military officials of the Dominican Republic that they were no longer in a position to guarantee the safety of American and foreign nationals and to preserve law and order" (ibid., 465).

But once the stranded civilians had been "rescued," Johnson needed a further justification for sending in even more troops; so he went on to shift his emphasis in justifying the intervention from stranded American citizens to illusory communist infiltrators: "[T]here are signs that people trained outside the Dominican Republic are seeking to gain control. Thus the legitimate aspirations of the Dominican people and most of their leaders for progress, democracy, and social justice are threatened and so are the principles of the inter-American system" (ibid.). The following day, Johnson stated of the Dominican situation: "We intend to carry on the struggle against tyranny no matter in what ideology it cloaks itself" (ibid., 467).

By May 2, the president no longer minced his words:

> The revolutionary movement [in the Dominican Republic] took a tragic turn. Communist leaders, many of them trained in Cuba, seeing a chance to increase disorder, to gain a foothold, joined the revolution. They took increasing control. And what began as a popular democratic revolution, committed to democracy and social justice, very shortly moved and was taken over and really seized and placed into the hands of a band of Communist conspirators. (Ibid., 471)

In support of Johnson's claims, his administration released a list of the names of fifty-three "known communists" in the Dominican Republic—a list that had little credibility among journalists as the following discussion demonstrates:

> DAN KURZMAN, *Washington Post:* "When American reporters pushed the American embassy for evidence that the Communists were taking over, they finally agreed to give us a whole list."

> TAD SZULD, *New York Times:* "No, they didn't agree, they forced it on us."

> KURZMAN: "Okay. Well, first they gave us a list of fifty-three hard-core Communists. Later they gave us a thirteen-page treatise."

> JOHN BARNES, *Newsweek:* "Which they had distributed in the U.S. before."

> KURZMAN: "Apparently, so we couldn't check it on the spot. And then we started checking it. I found that of the three who were supposed to have been given jobs by the Caamaño government [a previous Dominican regime, from which a number of the rebel leaders came], one turned out to be a die-hard conservative, another was a naval officer known to be a conservative, and another—"

SZULC: "One of them was ten years old."

KURZMAN: "No, let's not exaggerate. He was fifteen years old, and he'd never had an official job." (Quoted in Goldman, 1968: 396–97; brackets in original).

And so goes the official story of U.S. involvement in the Dominican Revolution of 1965. What the United States did with the help of twenty-three thousand troops was to rescue the revolution from the "other and dangerous hands," the "other evil forces," the "international conspiracy," the "band of Communist conspirators" that would have ushered in "another Communist government in the Western Hemisphere" (Johnson, 1966: 471). In a dramatic moment of President Johnson's May 2 speech, he quoted President Kennedy's words, "We in this hemisphere must also use every resource at our command to prevent the establishment of another Cuba in this hemisphere" (ibid., 472).

But precisely what resources the United States still had at its command in the wake of its dephallusization in its encounter with Castro's Cuba was very much at issue in President Johnson's policies—if not denotatively, then connotatively, if not consciously, then unconsciously. These aspects of the U.S. policy toward the Dominican Republic were to express themselves in shades of white and blue.

White as a Ghost

Reflecting on when he first heard of the troubles in the Dominican Republic in April 1965, President Johnson told members of the National Security Council:

> It's just like the Alamo. Hell, it's like if you were down at that gate, and you were surrounded, and you damn well needed somebody. Well, by God, I'm going to go—and I thank the Lord that I've got men who want to go with me, from [Secretary of Defense Robert S.] McNamara right on down to the littlest private who's carrying a gun. (Quoted in Goldman, 1968: 395)

There would be no white flag of surrender from this Texas volunteer who commanded the armed forces of the United States. He would send them full force to defend the interests of the underdogs, this time the democratic Dominicans fighting for their lives against the corrupt communists.

Johnson's decision would mean there would still be red in the region, but it would be the red of American blood sacrificially offered for the sake of justice, for the sake of democracy, for the sake of U.S. hegemony. Following from this sacrifice, it seemed that the United States expected it could white out the turbulent troubles of communism and restore the Caribbean to a seemingly color-free, white zone much like the one the U.S. Marines were establishing around embassy row in downtown Santo Domingo to keep the communists—if they were communists—out. Whatever it took, the Johnson administration was determined to keep the Dominican Republic from falling to the communists and to restore America's unquestioned hegemony in the region.

The themes of return and restoration are strong ones in the Dominican invasion. How they cast their shadow over the eastern half of the island of Hispaniola is very much in a ghostly form reminiscent of the refracted cinematic space of Vietnam. Whether in Rambo films or the many horror films about Vietnam POWs and MIAs, one aspect of America's psychic fixation on the Vietnam War is "the fantasy of the always-imminent-yet-deferred return"—of victory, of lost men, of masculinity (Howell, 1996: 298). So, too, is this fantasy found in the cracked Caribbean Sea/See; for, since the U.S. split from Castro's Cuba, the Caribbean Sea/See itself has been split, revealing the U.S. body politic as a body in pieces—a body more specifically without a phallus. In the Dominican Republic in 1965, the United States unwittingly set itself on a course of frustrated hope, of always waiting for what it had lost to be returned to it—its fully functioning phallus and the sense of hegemonic masculinity that comes with it. The U.S. invasion of the Dominican Republic, then, might be read, like the American public's fascination with Vietnam horror films, as "symptomatic of not only the desire to disown the injuries of Vietnam [and Cuba] but also the fascination exerted by those losses and the compulsion to repeat them [in the Dominican Republic]" (ibid.).

Unlike the American body politic of the 1980s, however, which was aware of what it had lost in Vietnam—a war and an untroubled sense of masculinity—this same body was unaware of what it had lost in the Caribbean in the early 1960s. Yes, Cuba had been lost to Castro and to Communism. But with this knowledge also existed a nonknowledge—of what the United States lost in losing Cuba. Consciously, the United States was sure that it did not want to suffer the loss of "another Cuba." Unconsciously, it fought to deny having lost a part of itself. When America's losses found expression at all, they were in ghostly or ghoulish forms, often appearing as if in dreams.

The recurrent dream that President Johnson reported having when he graduated from high school fits this pattern well. The dream goes like this: President Johnson was

> sitting alone in a small cage. The cage was completely bare, he said, except for a stone bench and a pile of dark, heavy books. As he bent down to pick up the books, an old lady with a mirror in her hand walked in front of the cage. He caught a glimpse of himself in the mirror and to his horror he found that the boy of fifteen had suddenly become a twisted old man with long, tangled hair and speckled, brown skin. He pleaded with the old woman to let him out, but she turned her head and walked away. (Kearns, 1976: 40)

Johnson reported this dream to Doris Kearns sometime during the last five years of his life, and Kearns records her skepticism about the authenticity of the dream. She writes:

> The dream is almost too good, too easy to fit into the pattern of his other dreams [that express castration anxiety]. It is without jagged edges, the false doors, blank spaces, and swerves that usually complicate our memories of dreams. I wondered as Johnson described it to me whether he was telling it in part for my sake.... There is no way of knowing. (Ibid., 40–41; my insertion)

If "authentic," Johnson's dream seemingly foreshadows the non-knowledge Johnson carried as president in his relationship with the Caribbean Sea/See—that sometimes things go awry. Sometimes the womanly mirror of the Caribbean Sea/See spitefully reflects and refracts the United States as an old, unkept, racially othered, and impotent man. In this Caribbean mirror/prism, the United States really does look like Uncle Sam—old and grey, a mere shadow of his former hegemonic self.

If "unauthentic," Johnson's dream might express the reflections turned refractions of a former president who left office a political ghost, unable to do what he had made his political career doing—constructing a consensus upon which he could, in this case, rally public opinion in support of his Vietnam policies and run for a final term in office. Rather than foreshadowing a coming castration, Johnson's dream on this reading tells Kearns what she and every American already "know." The fatal knowledge that ended Johnson's presidency was that Johnson was unable to restore himself or America to the place of loved objects. Faced with this failure, Johnson rereads himself and recognizes his own symbolic castration—a castration that occurred in Vietnam (and Cuba before it) and that was symbolically reenacted in the prismatically parallel Dominican Republic.

This second interpretation of Johnson's dream also symbolically reinscribes the U.S. fear of the dreaded "domino effect." Coined by President Eisenhower in reference to events in Southeast Asia, the domino effect came to be understood as follows: "when one nation falls to communism the impact is such as to weaken the resistance of other countries and facilitate, if not cause, their fall to communism" (*FRUS, 1964–1968*, 1: 484–85). Implicit in America's fear of the domino effect is its knowledge that it can lose its global hegemony piece by piece, country by country. What the United States did not count on, however, was losing a piece of itself, of being bound up in the contagious cycle of castration and being left with nothing but a phantom phallus. Thus, the second reading of President Johnson's "castration anxiety" dream suggests that in his twilight years he was able to acknowledge something that neither he nor the U.S. body politic could confront during the early 1960s—their symbolic loss of phallic power. Instead of rereading itself through the cycle of castration, the United States chose to deny its symbolic castration in the early 1960s. It attempted to exorcise the red communist/castration ghost it encountered this time in the Dominican Republic, but it was never able to white it out completely, for U.S. denial occurred not in white but in shades of blue.

Melancholy Blue(s)

President Johnson wrote in his memoirs, "The most important foreign policy problem I faced was that of signaling to the world what kind of man I was and what sort of policies I intended to carry out" (L. B. Johnson, 1971: 22). Whether judging by his Vietnam or Dominican Republic policies, most accounts suggest that he failed in this respect. In the Dominican Republic, for example, he alienated hemispheric partners in the Organization of American States (OAS) by making unilateral policy decisions that drew OAS members into an intervention that most opposed. Furthermore, the president's "irrelevant rationalizations and often inaccurate reconstruction of events [concerning the Dominican invasion], conspired to turn an essentially unmanageable and, in some ways, unavoidable crisis in a fundamentally unstable and crisis-prone Caribbean nation into a crisis of confidence in the President himself" (Geyelin, 1966: 237). President Johnson's handling of the Dominican affair resulted in "what was probably the lowest ebb in Lyndon Johnson's standing as a world statesman in all of the first two years or more of his Presidency" (ibid.).

"Low standing" was not the policy effect the president had been after. Instead, what Johnson desperately attempted to convey with his Dominican policy was that he was a man with a phallus and that the American body politic itself could be rephallusized under his leadership in the aftermath of its contagious contact with Castro's Cuba. The Dominican invasion should have been a blueprint for American success elsewhere in the world—in Vietnam, for instance. In the deep blue sea of the Caribbean, the American body politic should have found itself "standing tall" once again. It had gone to the Dominican Republic to fight for a better hemisphere. Indeed, it sent the U.S. naval carrier *Boxer* to land the Marines and escort American civilians to safety.

And yet somehow the Johnson administration's efforts were disturbingly off-color. Even though the president declared that his intentions in the Dominican invasion were the same as those of U.S. Senator Huey Long in his support of a Arkansas female senatorial candidate— "All I went to Arkansas [the Dominican Republic] for was to pull those big, pot-bellied politicians [communists] off this poor little woman's neck" (L. B. Johnson, 1966: 481; my insertions)—international opinion still feared that this was no way to treat a lady. President Johnson's policy was viewed not as chivalry but as indecent, as a sort of blue joke in which the blue hues of the Caribbean Sea were dishonorably treated, for his declarations of protection for the Dominican Republic were first and foremost cast in terms of protecting U.S. citizens and implicitly as protecting U.S. hemispheric interests. As one commentator noted, "Johnson seemed to be declaring that U.S. troops would land anywhere, anytime that a local conflict brought danger to American civilians in the area" (Geyelin, 1966: 239). From a Caribbean perspective, this policy was obscene. The president was asserting his and the American body politic's virility to the point of leaving them both overexposed (if indeed they had anything left to expose).

Even though the Johnson administration claimed victory in its quarantining of Castro's communism in the Caribbean, America was not rephallusized as a result of the Dominican intervention. America's rephallusization was not a simple matter of containing its losses to communism; it was also a matter of restoring itself as a loved object. Such a restoration would mean that the United States could once again see the masculine, hegemonic ideal of itself reflected back to it in the deep, blue Caribbean Sea/See. And yet only a few days after the Dominican invasion, President Johnson knew his Caribbean revisionings had not been achieved. He declared, "Now I am the most denounced man in the world" (L. B. Johnson, 1966: 480).

President Johnson, like the American body politic, had been stripped of his status as a loved object. As such, he and the American body politic that he saw reflected/refracted in the Caribbean Sea/See were bodies unable to communicate who they were (virile, phallic, hegemonic) or how they felt or hoped to feel (symbolically restored). These bodies not only were no longer assured the last word in hemispheric affairs; they seemed to be at a loss for meaningful words altogether.

In this respect, these symbolically castrated bodies resembled bodies in physical pain because, as Elain Scarry explains, "[p]hysical pain has no voice" (Scarry, 1985: 3). Like castration that "can neither be assumed nor denied, but only enacted" (B. Johnson, 1980: 12), "pain comes unsharably into our midst as at once that which cannot be denied and that which cannot be confirmed" (Scarry, 1985: 4). Voiceless, even ghostlike, "Physical pain does not simply resist language but actively destroys it, bringing about an immediate reversion to a state anterior to language, to the sounds and cries a human being makes before language is learned" (ibid.).

The "physical" pain of symbolic castration seemingly sent the wounded American body politic through the Lacanian looking glass of the Caribbean Sea/See out of the Symbolic (the realm of language) back into the Imaginary (the prelinguistic). For the U.S. body, this was a painful passage, for it involved a loss of guaranteed meaning that this Symbolic, specular space once provided. It was a voyage that simultaneously confirmed and denied America's phallic loss—of meaning, of omnipotence, of the last word. It is as an anguished howling—a macabre melancholia—that the American body politic "voiced" the bodily loss of its phallus and confronted its narcissistic wound.

In its attempt to deny and annul the pain of disappointed love it suffered in losing Cuba, the American body politic symbolically mirrored melancholia in its relations with the Dominican Republic in the early 1960s. The American body politic, in other words, suffered a severe case of the blues because of its loss of regional omnipotence.

Melancholia, like mourning, is the response to the loss of a loved object that produces symptoms of sadness and withdrawal from the world. Yet melancholia and mourning involve different ways of processing this loss, in part because the loss itself is different in each case. Mourning occurs in response to an actual loss of a loved object. As Freud puts it, "Reality-testing has shown that the loved object no longer exists" (1984: 253). In other words, generally the object has died. Melancholia, in contrast, involves "a loss of a more ideal kind. The object has not perhaps actually died, but has been lost as an object of love (e.g. in the case of a betrothed girl who has been jilted)" (ibid.), or, in the case of the United States, loss of a feminized Cuba.

Although the mourner knows who and what s/he has lost, the melancholic lacks a language to express his or her loss. This follows from the melancholic's inability to "see clearly what it is that has been lost...he knows *whom* he has lost but not *what* he has lost in him" (ibid., 254). The United States, for example, knew it lost Cuba, but it could not appreciate what else it lost in losing Cuba. Both the mourner and the melancholic know what external love object they have lost; however, because the mourner does not identify with the loved object in the same way as the melancholic, the melancholic loses something more with the loss of the object than does the mourner—a part of the self. In melancholia, the subject is fragmented.

Freud suggests that the process of melancholia involves a narcissistic identification between the melancholic and the lost object. In loving the lost object, the melancholic is loving himself or herself. In loving Cuba, the United States was loving itself by having fallen in love with its masculine, hegemonic reflection. This is narcissistic love in its purest form, for recall that "Narcissus drowns in his own reflection, never understanding that it is a reflection. The point of the story is not that Narcissus falls in love with himself but, since he fails to recognize his own reflection, that he lacks any conception of the difference between himself and his surroundings" (Lasch, 1991: 241).

This narcissistic identification of the melancholic with the loved/ lost object means that the melancholic has invested his or her ego in the loved/lost object. To lose the loved object, then, is to lose a part of one's ego. This explains why "[t]he melancholic displays something else besides which is lacking in mourning—an extraordinary diminution in his self-regard, an impoverishment of his ego on a grand scale. In mourning it is the world which has become poor and empty; in melancholia it is the ego itself" (Freud, 1984: 254). Or, as President Johnson put it, "Now I am the most denounced man in the world" (L. B. Johnson, 1966: 480).

In the process of mourning, the mourner "withdraw[s] from its attachments to the object," thereby embarking on the road to recovery. But because the melancholic's love for the lost object is a form of self-love—of narcissistic love—the melancholic does not give up the loved object even after it has been "lost." Had the United States given up on winning back Cuba, or at the least on reconstructing the cracked Caribbean Sea/See, it would have lost the possibility to once more see its masculine, hegemonic identity reflected back to it in this idealized feminine space. To give up on Cuba and the Caribbean, then, would be to lose a part of the self—U.S. phallic power, the U.S. phallus. Thus, "in spite of the conflict with the loved person the love-relationship need not be given up" (Freud, 1984: 258). A split of sorts occurs between what the melancholic allows himself or herself to know. Consciously, the United States knows that it has lost the loved object— Cuba. But unconsciously, it does not allow itself to know what it has lost in losing the loved object—a symbolically functioning phallus.

It is this conscious/unconscious knowledge split that accounts for the seemingly contradictory symptoms that melancholics sometimes exhibit. In response to their conscious loss and continued love of the object, they suffer this loss as well as attempt to make the lost object pay for the pain they are suffering. As a consequence, they themselves often experience extreme fear of punishment. Unconsciously, the melancholic denies the ego loss that accompanies loss of the loved object.

All of these symptoms presented themselves in the United States' relationship with the Caribbean region in the early 1960s. Symbolically castrated by Castro's Cuba, the American body politic under the Kennedy administration acknowledged the loss of Cuba but not its own loss of the phallus. At the same time that President Kennedy accepted responsibility for bungling the Bay of Pigs invasion, for instance, he simultaneously embarked on a series of policies (from economic embargoes to attempted assassinations of Castro) to make Castro's Cuba pay for having scorned America's love. But the United States feared repercussions in the region. Cuban-style communism might spread as easily as a row of dominoes fell. America might find its southern section swallowed up in a Communist lake. It might be the Alamo all over again, but this time it would be a red flag rising in victory. This really would be an extreme form of punishment and humiliation.

Sadly for President Johnson, America's symptomatic suffering of the always-imminent-yet-deferred return of its phallic power continued in the aftermath of the Dominican invasion. Even regional victory over the communists was not enough to erase the ego/phallic loss the United States experienced as a result of this invasion, for the president "knew" himself to be both hated and politically impotent. The U.S. Dominican strategy of at least unconsciously denying its loss of hegemonic masculinity and the phallic power that accompanies it only led the United States into deeper and deeper shades of blue... until they almost seemed purple.

America's "True" Color(s)

There are colorful ironies about the flag-waving rhetoric surrounding the Johnson administration's Dominican invasion. The first is that the very thing that the president, in defending his Dominican policy, claimed gave him such pride—the flying of the U.S. flag over a foreign country—was the source of his first "Caribbean test." When a group of U.S. high school students in the Panama Canal Zone decided to patriotically fly their flag outside their school, they "set into motion events that soon threatened our relations with Panama and endangered operation of the Panama Canal" (L. B. Johnson, 1971: 180). For a short time, the Canal Zone was under fire, Panama suspended diplomatic relations with the United States, and talks to begin renegotiation of the Canal treaties began. Old Glory, then, was a symbol not only of pride but of the high price the United States had to pay for not being loved as much by others as it was by its own.

The second irony involves the administration's prismatic use of policy rhetoric. It is reminiscent of the slogan about the American flag that was popularized in the 1990 Persian Gulf War: "These colors will not run." Indeed, the administration's prismatic strategy of covering (communist) red with (ghostly) white and then with (melancholic) blue ensured that, even when viewed collectively, each of America's primary colors remained separate.

Yet, the Johnson administration's strategy also ironically foreshadows the coming queer compensatory strategies the United States would rely on for its phallic recovery in its invasions of Panama and Haiti. In these later invasions, the red, white, and blue of the American flag are returned to the United States by the Caribbean Sea/See/Screen in that lascivious shade of lavender the United States so hoped to divert its eyes from in the aftermath of its contagion by Castro's Cuba. With the Clinton administration's invasion of Haiti, lavender even becomes an empowering U.S. color. But U.S. presidents have a long way to go before accepting such a colorfully mixed foreign-policy position. There is yet another strategy of denial (simulation) and another phallus (a simulated phallus) to try on before fitting America's body politic with a queer one. It is this simulated supplement that President Reagan dons in his invasion of Grenada.

4. LIGHTS, CAMERA, ... REAGAN; OR, FINDING THE REST OF AMERICA IN GRENADA

The same year the United States invaded the Dominican Republic in a "firm" denial of its phallic loss, Ronald Reagan published a book titled *My Early Life; or, Where's the Rest of Me?* In the opening chapter, Reagan explains the subtitle of the book—the title by which the book is now popularly known. In 1941, Reagan explains, he played the part of "Drake McHugh, the gay blade who cut a swathe among the ladies" in a film titled *King's Row.* The key scene of the film is the one in which Reagan/Drake—in bed after having suffered an accident in a railroad yard—awakes to discover that both of his legs have been amputated up to his hips by "a sadistic doctor (who disapproved of my dating his daughter and felt it was his duty to punish [castrate?] me)" (Reagan, 1965: 4; my insertion). Reagan is to express the "total shock" Drake experiences in the five words, "Where's the rest of me?" Writes Reagan of the challenge of pulling off this scene, "A whole actor would find such a scene difficult; giving it the necessary dramatic impact as half an actor was murderous. I felt I had neither the experience nor the talent to *fake it.* I simply had to find out how it really felt, short of actual amputation" (ibid.; my emphasis).

The future president did find out, albeit "under different circumstances than make-believe" (ibid., 6). Some five years later, a restless Reagan disillusioned by the personal isolation he felt as a movie actor, asked himself this same question. "Seeing the [movie] rushes, I could barely believe the colored shadow on the screen was myself. Possibly this was the reason I decided to find the rest of me" (ibid.) — in drama, sports, and politics.

It was in the field of politics that Reagan, acting as a symbolic substitute for the American body politic, was to "live" the latent content of his cinematic concern. Reagan did so by both asking for this American body, "Where's the rest of me?" and by supplying it with an answer in the form of a simulated supplement — the big stick America had been looking for since its encounter with Castro's Cuba. U.S. politics in the 1980s starred Ronald Reagan coming to the rescue, not just of Grenada (as he would later claim) but of America; for it was Reagan's simulated screen presence that presented the American body politic with a way of recovering its phallic power — the rest of America — and of restoring itself as a loved object in the Caribbean, if primarily for its own citizenry.

This was not a task accomplishable by the three presidents who preceded Reagan. Richard Nixon's foreign-policy preoccupations were in Southeast Asia, but when he ventured into Latin America the results were much the same as they had been for this former vice president on his 1958 tour of South America — plagued with anti-Americanism and mutual misunderstandings. Having moved away from the economic incentives of the Kennedy administration's Alliance for Progress, President Nixon's Latin American foreign policy was characterized by some as "benign neglect" (see Kryzanek, 1985: 63), except when it came to containing communism.

Yet even here President Nixon ran into difficulties. His covert destabilization of the democratic Marxist government of Salvador Allende in Chile, for example, succeeded in overthrowing the Allende government but spread this instability to the Nixon administration in the form of domestic and international criticism. Castration, to recall Barthes, is contagious. "[T]he value system and ethical standards that helped to foster the Watergate crisis" and its symbolic castration of the President were linked to U.S. involvement in Chile (ibid., 65). Writes Seymour Hersh:

> With Chile as with Watergate, cover-up payments were sought for CIA contacts and associates who were caught in the acts of crime. With Chile as with Watergate, records were destroyed and documents distorted. With Chile as with Watergate, much of the official testimony provided to congressional investigating committees was perjury. With Chile as with Watergate, the White House was in league with unscrupulous and violent men. (Hersh, 1983: 638)

The Nixon presidency, far from rephallusizing America or restoring it as a loved object in the Caribbean and Latin America, instead resulted in a further deepening of U.S. doubts about its president, the presidency, and itself.

President Gerald Ford, the only person to serve as U.S. president who was elected to neither that office nor the vice presidency, lacked both the time and the credibility to do anything other than hold on to his office until his electoral defeat to Jimmy Carter in 1976.

President Carter restored a sense of morality to the office of the presidency, with his emphasis on "high principle, human compassion, belief in negotiation, and a reluctance to intervene in leftist revolutions" (Kryzanek, 1985: 66–67). Even so, as president he did not succeed in making U.S. citizens feel good about themselves (something he was more successful at as a postpresident). This was the president who, for the sake of principles, negotiated the "giveaway" of the Panama Canal and who, in the interest of improved relations with Cuba, welcomed the Mariel boat people, of whom many were Cuban prisoners and mental patients. President Carter seemed to care more about his and the U.S. image abroad than he did about the U.S. people, a view seemingly confirmed when he remarked, "The hardest thing for the American people to understand is that we are not better than other people" (Kegley and Wittkopf, 1997: 9). This was not what the U.S. citizenry wanted to hear.

So, when Ronald Reagan burst onto the American political scene/ screen in his bid for the presidency, voters were all too willing to listen. This presidential candidate made it very clear where he stood, what he stood for, and what he stood against. He reminded the electorate that he had opposed the "giveaway" of the Panama Canal, and he extolled to them the evils of President Carter's foreign policy. This policy of " 'vacillation, appeasement and aimlessness' was bringing dishonor and humiliation 'all over the world' " (Destler, 1983: 129). This was not the sort of policy that would help America recover from its problematic past. America had to "exorcise the 'Vietnam syndrome,' " which Reagan "defined as a national sense of uncertainty, involving extreme reluctance to revert to military force" (Dumbrell, 1997: 5).

Running on the slogan "America Is Back!" candidate Reagan slipped into what was left of the dephallusized American body politic and made it appear whole again. The "Great Communicator" recovered America's voice and set out "to help Americans rise above pessimism by renewing their belief in themselves" (Erickson, 1985: 2). According to Ronald Reagan, America had not been emasculated in Cuba or Vietnam. Rather, "the Vietnam War was a 'noble cause' which our government had been 'afraid to win' " (Destler, 1983: 129). Under President Reagan, America would no longer be held hostage — either by the Iranian government, which permitted the detention of U.S. embassy personnel in the wake of its revolution, or by its own psychic wounds suffered in Cuba and Vietnam. Indeed, the mere swearing in of President Reagan was all it seemed to take to free the American hostages in Iran.

Ronald Reagan's symbolic capital was — like his "big stick" — enormous. As the newly elected president proved following his attempted assassination by John Hinckley Jr., he was a man who could take a bullet and recover from his wounds. Reagan's presidency made the American body politic believe it could do the same. Asking itself "Where's the rest of me?" the American body politic found its answer in Ronald Reagan, whose election some believed "marked the end of a national identity crisis through which the United States had been passing for some ten or fifteen years" (Kirkpatrick, 1983: 12).

Simulating

There is more than a bit of irony in Ronald Reagan's recovery of America's phallic identity, for identity confusion has always seemed to be a part of Ronald Reagan. One could never be sure if the film actor turned politician who succeeded in capturing the presidency was being himself or playing a role from one of his B movies. Asked during his first gubernatorial campaign what kind of governor he would make, he replied, "I don't know, I've never played a governor" (Cannon, 1982: 20). As president, Reagan was forever quoting movie lines in his speeches and presenting movie scenes as if they were "actual" incidents (Rogin, 1987: 7–8). Reagan lost himself in his movies and in his movie image. As a screen image, President Reagan did not mirror American identity. He screened it:

> A mirror requires both a referent and its reflection; it is dependent on outside standards to supply a reality check. . . . But the screen . . . takes the place of a mirror. It obliterates the referent: a self who sees himself from all angles [as Reagan did when he saw himself on screen] disappears into his image. Self-sufficient, the screen dispenses both with external history and with the historically formed human interior (for which the mirror reflection was often a symbol). When the camera brought Reagan's self inside the screen, to exist as an observed outside, it shattered the distinction between inside and outside. (Ibid., 6–7; my insertion)

With Ronald Reagan, the line between inside and outside, fact and fantasy, the real and the fake, was never clearly established. Yet, Reagan appeared authentic to the U.S. public because he always acted himself (Wills, 1987: 1). Reagan's presence embodied what Jean Baudrillard called simulation. Simulation "is no longer a question of imitation. . . . It is rather a question of substituting signs of the real for the real itself" (Baudrillard, 1983: 4). Simulation plays with appearances to fool the eye into believing that what is screened is "real." Reagan's presidency was symbolically saturated to the point where the president consistently substituted his screened image (as he did at the 1984 Republican National Convention) or his screen image (a character from a film role) for himself. Whether making a whole man appear to be half (Reagan as Drake McHugh) or half a nation appear whole (Reagan as America's symbolic phallus), Ronald Reagan maneuvered a symbolic substitution between screen images and "real" images. Masking the absence of the real by substituting signs of the real for the real itself, Reagan assured Americans that America was back. America's dephallusization had been but "a temporary aberration. There is a spiritual revival going on in this country, a hunger on the part of the people to once again be proud of America, all that it is and all that it can be.... The era of self-doubt is over" (quoted in the *New York Times*, May 28, 1981, sec. iv: 20). Moving from "real" history to "reel" history, Reagan promised to win the "Vietnam War" (this time in Latin America) and to deny Cuba any further victories in the region. The "great American synecdoche," as Reagan has been called (Wills, 1987: 1), sampled his way through the Caribbean scene to creatively construct a Caribbean *screen* onto which American's hegemonic identity could once more be projected. This screen was none other than the projecting surface of the Caribbean Sea/See.

Steading

Having chiseled away at Castro's Cuba unsuccessfully for two decades, the American body politic changed its artistic inclination from sculptor to simulator under Reagan. Reagan's move from mirror to screen—from representing reality to simulating it—freed him and America from referentiality. There was no longer a need to recast the realities of U.S.–Caribbean relations in stone. Instead, what was called for was a more fluid strategy—a strategy that masked the absence of "real" American power by projecting positive images of America's phallic fortunes onto a feminized Caribbean Sea/See/Screen.

But the Reagan administration's strategy of fooling the American eye as to its phallic recovery would come to nothing if the screen/sea on which its heroic hegemonic identity was to feature was not steady enough to show this illusion faithfully. Yet everywhere President Reagan looked in the Caribbean, he saw turbulence. It took the form of a battle for survival between the United States and the "Evil Empire." No matter that the realities of Soviet economic overstretch had cooled the Cold War to its cracking point. Nor should America be deceived by Premier Mikhail Gorbachev's insistence that serious meddling in America's sphere of influence was not a priority for the soon-to-be-splitting-up Soviet Union. In place of Soviet assurances, Reagan projected a plethora of evil images. The Soviets, he claimed, sponsored the states of Cuba and Nicaragua and threatened the supposedly democratic government of El Salvador. The Soviets' twisted trajectory through the hemisphere threatened American regional security and hegemony. Without concerted efforts to roll back regional communism, Reagan warned Americans they might "see the map of Central America covered in a sea of red, eventually lapping at our own borders" (quoted in the *New York Times,* March 6, 1986). The imagined tides of communism had to be redirected. Pitting image against image, the Reagan administration deployed its own imaginary breaker in this battle, the Caribbean Basin Initiative (CBI).

Proposed in 1982, the CBI offered "one-way free trade, investment incentives, increased economic and military aid, technical assistance to the private sector, and special help for Puerto Rico and the Virgin Islands" (Pastor, 1982: 1039). More important, it provided the administration with a capitalist container for its anticommunist security policies. The CBI was itself the creative result of another of Reagan's imaginary receptacles, the Caribbean Basin. Taking advantage of his antichameleon-like character — environments adapt themselves to Reagan rather than the other way around (Wills, 1987: 1) — Reagan discursively fused the Central American coastline with the Caribbean archipelago, two geopolitical locales that until 1982 had been dealt with (if only rhetorically) as separate foreign-policy concerns.

"The new cartographic definition of the region as a whole gave final expression to what had become a [simulated] political reality, the vision of the Caribbean Basin as a 'U.S. lake'" (Thorndike, 1989: 251; my insertion).

The "lake effect" of the CBI had the potential to improve the diplomatic climate in the region in two ways. First, the Caribbean Sea, like any fluid, takes the shape of the container into which it is placed. America's "backyard"—renamed the "front yard" by Reagan (*PPPRR*, January 21, 1983: 90)—was a morass with currents that could trap, confuse, and impede U.S. diplomats if these currents were not channeled in some clear direction. Flowing through the Caribbean Sea to and from the United States are oil and other natural resources, immigrants and refugees, narcotics, tourism, and (feared the Reagan administration) dreaded communism. Through this sea flows the very lifeblood of the United States. As Reagan put it, "The Caribbean region is a vital strategic and commercial *artery* for the United States" (ibid., February 16, 1982: 323; my emphasis) and it is "our lifeline to the outside world" (ibid., May 15, 1983: 450). The CBI— Reagan's corollary to the Monroe Doctrine (Ashby, 1988: 272)— promised political stability and economic development to the region as a way to encourage some flows (shipping and tourism), redirect others (immigration), and interrupt still others (narcotics and communism). Once enclosed within a basin, the turbulence produced by the mixing of these flows and the meeting of multicolored Caribbean rhythms could be managed. Contradictions could not be eliminated, but they could be contained. The Caribbean whirlpool could be cordoned off, reducing what might have become tidal waves within a sea to ripples on a lake. Without such precautions, the generative potential of the Caribbean region might breed unwanted communist offspring, thus further foiling America's attempt at rephallusization.

The Caribbean encoded as a site of generative possibilities precedes U.S. involvement in the region, as the following passage by Antonio Benítez-Rojo details:

Let's be realistic: the Atlantic is the Atlantic (with all its port
cities) because it was once engendered by the copulation of
Europe — that insatiable solar bull — with the Caribbean archipelago; the Atlantic is today the Atlantic (the navel of capitalism) because Europe, in its mercantilist laboratory, con-
ceived the project of inseminating the Caribbean womb with
the blood of Africa; the Atlantic is today the Atlantic (NATO,
World Bank, New York Stock Exchange, European Economic
Community, etc.) because it was the painfully delivered child
of the Caribbean, whose vagina was stretched between con-
tinental clamps . . . ; all Europe pulling on the forceps to help
at the birth of the Atlantic. . . . After the blood and salt water spurts, quickly sew up torn flesh and apply the antiseptic
tinctures, the gauze and surgical plaster; then the febrile wait
through the forming of a scar: suppurating, always suppurating. (Benítez-Rojo, 1992: 5)

The Caribbean as water, womb, woman attests to the virility of
the shorelines it borders, announcing their purpose, promise, and
promiscuity. Copulating couples of solids/fluids, empires/plantations,
men/women propagate signs engendered in this discourse as either masculine or feminine. Just as in psychoanalytic discourse in which the
term *woman* functions as a passageway (vagina) through which males
become mature subjects and as a receptacle (womb) that assures re-
production, the Caribbean signs of "woman" have functions but are
denied identities of their own. Woman (shipping lanes and colonies)
functions as the necessary complement to man (naval hegemons and
empires). According to Luce Irigaray, the feminine functions in psychoanalytic discourse as a "faithful, polished mirror" (1985a: 27) that reproduces masculine subjectivity but that is not itself representable.
Gazing into the mirror (woman and Caribbean Sea), male subjects (empires) see only themselves and not the mirror that generates their reflection. Of woman's place in this phallocentric system that offers her
a function but no identity, Irigaray suggests, "She has no 'proper'
name" (1985b: 26) other than that of the male (empire) she reflects
(French Guiana and Hispaniola).

Although there have been many complaints about the heterosexual and seemingly essentializing categories that may constrain Irigaray's argument (Schor, 1989; Berg, 1991), these objections do not detract from Irigaray's inventive speculation about the relationship between masculine and feminine categories. Irigaray argues that the masculine ability to penetrate and the feminine ability to reflect images correspond to a hierarchy of solids and fluids found in psychoanalytic theory as well as in physics. In both, visible forms (penis/mainland) are privileged over formless voids (vagina/water).

Irigaray's observation that gender is coded in terms of solids and fluids leads to her account of the potentially turbulent role the feminine may play in psychoanalytic discourse. The feminine as mirror only reflects masculine subjectivity if it is placid, unclouded, and fixed. Without a fixed feminine object, "the erection of the subject might thereby be disconcerted and risk losing its elevation and penetration. For what would there be to rise up from and exercise his power over? And in?" (Irigaray, 1985a: 133).

Although Irigaray's argument fixes the fluid character of woman in a heterosexual discourse as a mirror (more on this in the next chapter), her general observations on engendered codings of solids and fluids need not be constrained within a reflective (representational) discourse. As the filmic figure of Ronald Reagan demonstrates, seemingly solid masculine subjectivity can appear to "be" if projected onto a fluidly feminine screen. Like Irigaray's reflective pool/mirror, this cinematic space must also remain placid, unclouded, and fixed. Whereas Irigaray's discourse fixes feminine fluids as a mirror, Reagan's discourse symbolically fixes them as a screen onto which America's masculine subjectivity is simulated.

Returning to the connection between stability and hegemony found in U.S. foreign-policy discourse, and specifically to the second "lake effect" offered by the CBI, shoring up the Caribbean Sea/See/ Screen makes U.S. hegemonic subjectivity possible. Placing the Caribbean Sea into a basin contains and constrains a variety of flows, thus transforming a whirlpool into a lake *that is also a screen.* What the

Caribbean Sea/See/Screen (woman) screens is U.S. hegemonic subjectivity (man). If the feminine were to cease functioning as a simulating
screen, masculine subjectivity would be in crisis. Writes Irigaray, "Perhaps for the time being the serene contemplation of empire must be
abandoned in favor of taming those forces which, once unleashed,
might explode the very concept of empire" (ibid., 136). This is one
interpretation of U.S. actions in the invasion of Grenada.

Stepping Stones

Turbulent flows that threaten the placidity of the Caribbean come in
many varieties. In 1983, the United States feared disruptions from the
insemination of Central America and the Caribbean by its Eastern
bloc rival, the accompanying spread of the communist virus, and their
mixing in the spilling of blood in the Grenadian coup.

That the Reagan administration pronounced Grenada the center
of the Caribbean vortex was, if not predicted, at least foreshadowed
by the president's screen and rhetorical presences. As an actor, Reagan
was a star of B movies, not Hollywood blockbusters. Reagan could
make a spectacular splash in smaller picture such as *King's Row* or
with the small but significant part of George "The Gipper" Gipp in
The Knute Rockne Story. The scale of these roles never overshadowed
Reagan; rather, they were obscure enough to allow him to recycle himself and the American body politic through them without being called
on to measure his sampled screen subjectivities against "reality."

This could not be accomplished in bigger pictures. Reagan's attempts to turn the tide of communism in his epic action adventures in
Central America, the "obsessive heart of the administration's Third
World concerns" (Dumbrell, 1997: 80), never worked; for, in Central
America, the president remained burdened by accountability—for
the incremental investments of American money and personnel in the
secret war against the Nicaraguan Sandinista government and in U.S.
support of the military-backed Salvadoran government. Screening
America's phallic recovery in Grenada in 1983 allowed the Reagan

administration to highlight the importance of a big fight on a scale small enough for Reagan to star in. And, as we will see later, clips of America's triumph in Grenada could be used as trailers for many of Reagan's other planned pictures.

Rhetorically, Reagan played the communist card just as he had in his first starring anticommunist crusade, as president of the Screen Actors Guild. Speaking of "other dangers" in addition to economic and social challenges in his speech proposing the CBI, Reagan described communism as "a new kind of colonialism [that] stalks the world today and threatens our independence. It is brutal and totalitarian; it is not of our hemisphere, but it threatens our hemisphere, and has established footholds on American soil for the expansion of its colonialist ambitions" (*PPPRR*, February 16, 1982: 324). He continued: "A dark future is foreshadowed by the poverty and repression of Castro's Cuba, the tightening grip of the totalitarian left in Grenada and Nicaragua, and the expansion of Soviet-backed Cuban-managed support for violent revolution in Central America" (ibid.).

Warned Reagan, "If we do not act promptly and decisively in defense of freedom, new Cubas will arise from the ruins of today's conflicts. We will face more totalitarian regimes, tied militarily to the Soviet Union; more regimes exporting subversion" (ibid., 325). Should such events transpire, U.S. regional and global hegemony would be threatened. In another speech, Reagan explained:

> If Central America were to fall, what would the consequences be for our position in Asia, Europe and for alliances such as NATO? If the United States cannot respond to a threat near our own borders, why should Europeans or Asians believe that we are seriously concerned about threats to them? If the Soviets can assume that nothing short of an actual attack on the United States will provoke an American response, which ally, which friend will trust us then? (Ibid., May 15, 1983: 453)

This domino dynamic as applied to the Caribbean Basin led the Reagan administration to conclude that the Caribbean's "eruptions of gases and lava" (Benítez-Rojo, 1992: 26) had formed the island of

Grenada into another "stepping stone" on communism's route to the United States (Thorndike, 1989: 251). Just before becoming president, Reagan had expressed his concerns in a radio address, warning that "the Caribbean is rapidly becoming a Communist lake in what should be an American pond" (quoted in Dugger, 1983: 518). Whether events in Grenada led to the reddening of the Caribbean or simply stirred up communist influences in the region, the result would be the same for the United States. The Caribbean would cease to simulate U.S. hegemony and thus deny it a sense of subjectivity. According to President Reagan: "Grenada, that tiny little island — with Cuba at the west end of the Caribbean, Grenada at the east end — that tiny little island is building now, or having built for it, on its soil and shores, a naval base, a superior air base, storage bases and facilities for the storage of munitions, barracks, and training grounds for the military" (*PPPRR*, March 10, 1983: 373). This led Reagan to conclude, "It isn't nutmeg that's at stake in the Caribbean and Central America. It is the United States['] national security" (ibid.). It is the U.S. sense of identity.

Should there have been any doubt that U.S. identity was masculinely inscribed in the region, Maurice Bishop — the prime minister of Grenada who was murdered in the coup that prompted the U.S.-led invasion — made the link in colloquial terms. In October 1982, after Bishop delivered his famous "We Are Nobody's Backyard" speech in response to U.S. pressures to break ties with Cuba, Bishop accepted Cuban technicians and arms. Commenting on these events to Robert Pastor, Bishop remarked, "We are a lot like Americans. If you kick us in the shins, we will kick you in the balls" (quoted in Pastor, 1990: 13).

Reagan picked up on this theme in his own comments about the need to defend U.S. national security in the Caribbean Basin: "Teddy Roosevelt is known to have said, 'Speak softly and carry a big stick.' Well, there are plenty of soft speakers around, but that's where the similarity ends" (*PPPRR*, May 20, 1983: 43). America, Reagan implied, was the only regional power with a "big stick."

The Reagan administration feared that Grenada was becoming the big stick of the Soviet Union and Cuba. Displaying photos during his "Star Wars" speech of the 9,800-foot-long airport runway under construction in Grenada, Reagan commented: "The rapid buildup of Grenada's military potential is unrelated to any conceivable threat to this island country of under 110,000 people and totally at odds with the pattern of other eastern Caribbean States, most of which are unarmed. The Soviet-Cuban militarization of Grenada, in short, can only be seen as *power projection* into the region" (ibid., March 23, 1983: 440; my emphasis).

To guard against the conception of more Soviet-Cuban offspring in the Caribbean, the CBI offered Caribbean states both economic opportunities and "a defensive shield to protect [them] from Communist intervention while they go forward with economic reform" (ibid., August 13, 1983: 1157). But this defensive shield came too late for Grenada. The seeds of revolution had been planted in 1979. The best the Reagan administration could hope for at this point was a miscarriage (abortion, of course, being out of the question for this administration). Grenada, like Cuba, represented a small but significant puncture in the democratic diaphragm of the CBI. Neither state was slated to receive CBI benefits. Positioned at the edges of the Caribbean, they reminded the Reagan administration that the CBI was not a perfect fit.

Although the CBI placed an imaginary barrier between democratic and communist states in the region, it was not enough by itself to change the course of events in Grenada. The opportunity for decisive American action came in October 1983. When Prime Minister Bishop was put under house arrest and later executed by a faction of his own leftist New Jewel Party, the United States seized on these events to screen a dramatic "rescue mission." The Reagan administration first called on the steadying influences of the Organization of Eastern Caribbean States (OECS), a simulated "neighborhood" that "asked" for U.S. support in its efforts to reconsolidate the Caribbean coasts and still the headwaters of communism in the eastern Caribbean (Weber, 1995b: 92–112) From Bridgetown (yes, Bridgetown), the OECS with

Jamaica and Barbados issued a transparent "invitation" for United States military assistance. Reagan's spokesperson, Larry Speakes, wrote of the OECS invitation:

> What we were claiming was that the OECS had invited us to participate in the invasion. The truth of the matter is that on Sunday, October 23, the day the "invitation" was issued, a representative of President Reagan . . . was on hand at the OECS meeting in Bridgetown, Barbados — just to make sure that when the invitation was issued, it was sent to the right address. You might also say that we RSVP'ed in advance. (Speakes, 1988: 161)

But the "truth of the matter" was not at issue for the administration. Only appearances matter. And so the Reagan administration enthusiastically accepted its own invitation. The CBI was about to be refitted for the region.

Standing Tall

Two days after the United States led a multinational force into Grenada, President Reagan addressed the nation. "Grenada, we were told, was a friendly island paradise for tourism. Well," he continued, "it wasn't. It was a Soviet-Cuban colony, being readied as a major military bastion to export terror and undermine democracy. We got there just in time" (*PPPRR*, October 27, 1983: 1521). A feeling of urgency permeated U.S. foreign-policy discourse on Grenada, even finding expression in the U.S. code name for the invasion: Operation Urgent Fury. This makes sense considering that the military action in Grenada was in response to a hostage situation involving actual (democratic tradition of eastern Caribbean; see Selbin, 1993), potential (American medical students), and psychological (America defeated in Vietnam) victims. Speaking of events in Grenada, Reagan warned, "The nightmare of our hostages in Iran must never be repeated" (*AFPCD*, 1983: 1411). Nor should the United States remain caught in the grips of its Vietnam nightmare. In Grenada, the United States had used force decisively. In Grenada, it had not been "afraid to win" a victory against communism. In Grenada, it had freed itself from its "actual" history in Vietnam and from its symbolic phallic loss in its encounter with Castro's Cuba.

In the aftermath of the invasion, the administration once again sampled the Caribbean, this time to inscribe Operation Urgent Fury as an act of liberation. Said Reagan: "To call what we did in Grenada an invasion, as many have, is a slur and a misstatement of fact. It was a rescue mission, plain and simple" (*PPPRR*, November 13, 1983: 1595). Having inoculated the region against the virus of communism, the United States and its Caribbean allies transformed a communist stepping stone into a democratic breaker. The president expressed these sentiments in a speech to the Grenadian people in Saint George's three years after the invasion:

> There is a story, perhaps it's a legend, that in 1933 a group of young boys were in a swimming race across your harbor. And in the midst of the race, according to the story, to the horror of the crowd that watched, a shark appeared and surfaced directly under one young swimmer. For a few terrorizing minutes, the boy was carried on the back of the shark until the shark hit a wharf, and the boy was knocked to safety and pulled out of the water by his friends and neighbors. Well, dear people of Grenada, for a time it appeared that you were like that boy riding on the back of a shark. Your friends held their breath hoping and praying for you. And it was our honor to help you get off the shark. (Ibid., February 20, 1986: 238)

Securing this southern shoreline by calming the surge of communism enabled the United States to reclaim its most important hostage — its identity as a regional and global power. Gazing onto their Caribbean screen, U.S. policymakers once again saw their hegemonic identity projected. According to Representative Dick Cheney, because of U.S. success in Grenada "[a] lot of folks around the world feel we are more steady and reliable than before" (October 28, 1983; quoted in

Dunn and Watson, 1985: 172). Senator Rudy Boschwitz called the invasion "[a]n important extension of our national will" (October 29, 1983; quoted in ibid., 173). And President Reagan described it as "one of the highest of the high points of my eight years" (*PPPRR*, 1990: 458). Lest the inferences of these statements go undetected, Senator Lawton Chiles spelled them out: "At some stage there has to be some feeling that the United States is not totally impotent" (October 29, 1983; quoted in Dunn and Watson, 1985: 173). Reagan had succeeded in recovering America's phallic power and restoring America as a loved object for its own citizenry.

Returned to the community of democratic eastern Caribbean states, postinvasion Grenada sealed the southeastern lip of the Caribbean Basin. For this, the United States provided Grenada with CBI assistance and infrastructural rebuilding support, including the finances to complete its airport. What the invasion of Grenada offered the United States was a reservoir of foreign-policy signs into which Reagan would dip throughout his presidency.

Preinvasion Grenada became a testimony to how communist influences led to internal strife, a lesson directed toward Nicaragua. Commenting on the implications of Grenada, one Reagan administration official said, "I would like to believe that the *Commandantes* [of Nicaragua] are beginning to recognize that, when *diktat* and imposition replace democratic institutions and legal safeguards, political differences tend to degenerate into violence" (Deputy Secretary of State Kenneth W. Dam, November 14, 1983; *AFPCD*, 1983: 1269).

Postinvasion Grenada signified that although the communist virus was still festering in the region, the disease could be quarantined and those states that had fallen ill could be cured. President Reagan noted, "But what was happening in Grenada was not an isolated incident. The Soviet bloc and Cuba have been committing enormous resources to undermine our liberty and independence. Nowhere is this threat more pressing than in Nicaragua" (*PPPRR*, July 19, 1984: 1061). The president also remarked, "Looking around the world, in the past 4 years, not a single country has fallen to communism . . . but one nation has been set free from the clutches of Fidel Castro. I'm talking about Grenada" (ibid., July 26, 1984: 1095). And finally:

> We should learn the lesson of Grenada. My meeting with nine Caribbean leaders there showed me that they certainly have. One Caribbean Prime Minister summing up the discussions said, "Sometimes we wish we were a little closer to Central America so that we could give you more support. You're on the right course in Central America," he said, "and we're begging you not to give in and allow any more Communist beachheads to be established in this hemisphere." (Ibid., February 22, 1986: 245–46)

Thanks to the U.S.-led multinational invasion, Grenadians appeared to be empowered to make their own choices, even while the U.S. military occupied their nation-state: "[T]he collective action was undertaken to resolve a condition of anarchy, not to alter a functioning political system. . . . Indeed, what we found in Grenada suggests that Grenadians are now in a far better position to exercise their fundamental right of self-determination" (Deputy Secretary of State Kenneth W. Dam, November 14, 1983; *AFPCD*, 1983: 1268).

The invasion itself became the administration's narrative of a quick, efficient success that distracted the sign-consuming American public from both the prolonged and largely unsuccessful battle against communism in Nicaragua as well as the loss of U.S. Marines to a terrorist attack in Lebanon a few days earlier. In addition, the administration deployed this narrative to underscore moral aspects of U.S. foreign policy: "There is a fundamental moral distinction between the Grenada rescue mission and the Soviet invasion of Afghanistan—a brutal and bloody conquest that aims to destroy freedom, democracy and self-determination," said President Reagan. "It's the difference between totalitarianism and democracy, between tyranny and freedom" (*PPPRR*, October 24, 1984: 1637–38).

Overall, because of its success in rolling back the tide of regional communist influences in Grenada, the United States "stood for" something again. President Reagan commented:

We've been moving quickly these last 3½ years or so toward peace through strength. We know it's America's role in the world to stand for something. We need to be a reliable friend to our allies and a good neighbor to our friends nearby, and you can't be any of those things without strength. We always want everyone in the world to understand that Uncle Sam is a friendly old man, but he has a spine of steel. (Ibid., October 15, 1984: 1531)

The friendly old man turned president, Ronald Reagan, seemed to steel America's image of itself in ways it had been lacking since its encounter with Castro's Cuba. Playing in/on the scene/screen of simulation, Reagan paradoxically persuaded the American body politic that its supplemental simulated phallus was not just "reel" but "real." It could be backed up not just by "reel" images of U.S. hegemonic power but by the "real" itself—America's spine of steel. In this way, Reagan reassured the American body politic that it stood for good old representations of reality by fashioning these "representations" in a simulated style.

slipping

Halford Mackinder once wrote that the "ideal geographer" can, among other things "visualize the play and the conflict of the fluids over and around solid forms" (quoted in Tuathail, 1996). The same might be said of the "ideal foreign policymaker." Reagan administration officials attempted to live up to this ideal. With the Caribbean Basin Initiative as their solid frame, they did succeed (however briefly) in calming the cascade of conflicting interpretations of regional events and transforming the Caribbean into "the source and repository of many of mankind's noblest dreams. Our Caribbean Basin Initiative," explained President Reagan, "is a reflection of our commitment to sustaining those moral visions—or noble visions" (*PPPRR*, November 30, 1982: 1527). Gazing onto its Caribbean (feminine) screen, the United States temporarily solidified its claim as regional (masculine) hegemon, albeit in a simulated form.

For the Reagan administration, "The Caribbean Basin Initiative was a particularly promising sign" (Ronfeldt, 1983: 3). It made possible a tightly woven intertext of the Grenada invasion through the joining of foreign policy and geography. The channels of U.S.–Caribbean policy previously cut by the Monroe Doctrine and the Cold War found a fresh current in the CBI. Thanks to this, the U.S.-led invasion of Grenada was not just a regional dredging up of the East–West struggle. Rather, U.S. objectives in this struggle (containing communism, liberating oppressed peoples, etc.) were supplemented with North–South concerns (primarily economic development and dialogue on how to achieve development). The CBI encompassed both. Contextualized by the CBI, the "security shield" offered by the United States was necessary not as a goal in itself but as a means to economic development for participating Caribbean states. Grenada, then, was both a political and an economic battleground.

Even more important was the fact that the CBI can be read as a step by the United States toward "collective hegemony" in the region, with the invasion of Grenada read as the culmination of that process in the eastern Caribbean. Whether with respect to political, economic, or military concerns, the Reagan administration seemed to recognize that regional hegemony was not something it could accomplish unilaterally. Hegemony by definition is relational. Hegemony works best when simulated, when its appearance is manipulated so that a hegemon's "will" stands for the will of a dominated region. Writes one policy analyst:

> This [collective hegemony] would be feasible if other Caribbean Basin governments would collaborate with the United States as sovereign equals so that the framework's principles would advance the national interests of *all* partners. Other Basin governments would recognize that their own long-range security and development depend on promoting the stability and security of their neighbors, opposing the expansion of foreign (especially Soviet) military forces in the area, preventing the internationalization of local political strug-

gles, and restraining the use of military force by any Basin nation to settle local conflicts. (Ronfeldt, 1983: 51–52; emphasis in original)

Should its efforts to stabilize the Caribbean Basin and still the Caribbean Sea/See/Screen become a collective goal of the United States and CBI-aid recipients, "[t]he United States would be constrained from behaving like a hegemonic power, yet it could derive benefits as though hegemony existed" (ibid., 52). In other words, hegemony understood as the domination of one party by another would appear as if it had given way once again to the good-neighbor policy. President Reagan spoke of the CBI's security shield in these terms:

> Our Caribbean Basin Initiative is designed to help the nations there help themselves through trade and private investment. The Soviet and Cuban Caribbean Basin Initiative, on the other hand, is to brutally impose Communist rule and deny individual freedom.... Because of this aggression, we also support a security shield for the area. The security shield is very much like a Neighborhood Watch. The Neighborhood Watch is where neighbors keep an eye on each other's homes so outside troublemakers and bullies will think twice. Well, our policy in Central America is like a neighborhood watch. But this watch doesn't protect someone's silverware; it protects something more valuable—freedom (*PPPRR*, August 15, 1983: 1177)

Some two months after making these comments, Reagan broadened the "neighborhood watch" to the entire Caribbean Basin through the invasion of Grenada. Acting together, the OECS supplied simulated legitimacy and the United States supplied (and was simultaneously supplied with) a simulated big stick.

Although the Reagan administration—like so many administrations since President Monroe—persuasively argued for regional hegemony as the basis for global hegemony, the Caribbean seems to be an unlikely anchor for such a claim. As Benítez-Rojo reminds us, what the Caribbean signifies is the "impossibility of being able to assume a stable identity" (1992: 27) because the mestizo identity of the Caribbean is always already fragmented. What the Reagan administration did so successfully in Grenada was use this fragmentation to project a phallic image of itself onto the Caribbean screen and, from there, screen this imagery globally. Supplementing itself with the leadership of a fragmented film figure who made it appear whole, the American body in pieces found the rest of itself in Grenada.

Yet, Reagan's restoration of the American body politic's phallic power was short-lived. The CBI and the invasion of Grenada only managed to contain the confusing currents of the Caribbean for a short time. As suggested earlier, Reagan's simulating strategy ran into snags when he tried to fool the eyes of the American public into believing he should star in Central American features. These manipulations of appearances never worked, for all the American public saw on these screens were trailers for future Vietnams.

Referentiality and accountability remained for Reagan when he moved from B pictures to blockbusters because these roles were too well known to the American public to be differently portrayed by Reagan. Reagan's reinscriptions of his Central American policy as not another Vietnam, for example, were not accepted. Reagan's failures in gaining public and congressional support for his Central America sequels to Grenada ultimately cost the administration its symbolic capital and its simulated phallus. In 1986, the Iran–Contra scandal erupted, revealing that the administration had illegally diverted funds to the contras through the sale of arms to Iran. In the aftermath of Iran–Contra, Americans seemed less seduced by simulation and tended to crave "real" referentiality once more, all the while trying to fool their eyes that America's (simulated/"reel") phallus was really back.

These mixed desires are exemplified by President George Bush's activities in the U.S.-led invasion of Panama. As the first post–Cold War and post-Reagan president, Bush found himself drawing on empty signs (no longer East versus West but male versus female and masculine versus feminine) in foreign-policy performances that paled in comparison to those of his predecessor. Mixing referentiality and simulation as well as mirrors and screens in his foreign-policy rhetoric, it is not surprising that in Bush's bid to restore America's phallic power Bush also embarked on a mixing of America's sex, gender, and sexuality.

5. SOMETHING'S STILL MISSING

MALE HYSTERIA AND THE U.S. INVASION OF PANAMA

As Ronald Reagan faded from the American scene, his standby, Vice President George Bush, assumed the presidency. Unlike Reagan, who changed how Americans saw themselves, Bush was faulted for lacking the "vision thing." Bush did not project the same image of America as did his predecessor. Whereas Reagan appeared to be calm and self-assured (if a little confused), Bush seemed to be simultaneously combative and wimpish, even though he had a "real" record of heroic service in World War II. Reagan's projection of America was always singularly male and masculine, whereas Bush's America was mixed — both in terms of sex and gender and in terms of representation and simulation. Sometimes treating the Caribbean as a mirror and others as a screen, Bush used any tactic he could to maintain America's hegemonic image.

Caught somewhere within Reagan's fading simulations, the United States under Bush was unsure what image — and what sex and gender — it represented/projected. Doubts about America's phallic power reemerged in the form of national and international discourses on America's hegemonic decline. These debates in themselves testified to the effectiveness of Reagan's role in the early 1980s as the rest of America. But even Reagan could not fool the eye forever. As Iran–Contra broke and Reagan's presidential presence declined, so too did America's simulated hegemonic power.

And so, in a symbolic effort saturated with psychoanalytic subtexts to overcome the "wimp factor" and rerun America's simulated phallus onto the Caribbean Screen, George Bush turned to Panama. Substituting political rigidity for "real" phallic power (as he would later do in the run-up to the Persian Gulf War), on December 20, 1989, Bush ordered the United States to lead a multinational invasion of Panama to remove General Manuel Noriega from power. As a former CIA operative while Bush was director of that organization, Noriega overflowed with both signs of masculinity (in his defiance of Bush) and possible "truth" about America's covert covers in the region. So inscribed, Noriega threatened to unmask the simulation of Bush's masculine America as well as to overexpose the president himself. In this context, it is not surprising that, in analyzing the cause of the invasion, a White House adviser remarked that Bush "felt that Noriega was thumbing his nose at him" (Morton, 1990: 148). Read symptomatically through psychoanalytic discourse, Noriega's political gesture toward Bush amounts to a symbolic waving of Noriega's penis at the president (Rubenstein, 1993). Finding Noriega with his pants down, Bush could not ignore the temptation to let him have it. But Bush did not have "it" — in either a simulated or "real" form.

Bush compensated for America's fading phallic loss in much the same way President Johnson did in the invasion of the Dominican Republic: by boldly circulating signs of American masculinity. But grafted onto the wimpish body of George Bush, these signs did not appear to be simulated — to be a substitution "of signs of the real for the real itself" (Baudrillard, 1983: 4); for Bush could not convince anyone (apart from his wife, apparently) of his masculinity (Rubenstein, 1991). Instead, these circulating signs appeared to be unreal. Rather than creatively fooling America's eye as to its phallic endowments, Bush's attempt at hypermasculinity overexposed his (and America's) lacks. Seeping through the simulated screen of this post-Reagan presidency was a glimpse of America's legacy from its confrontation with Castro's Cuba—a castrated American body politic.

The Bush administration's invasion of Panama was designed to spectacularize America's simulated sense of manliness in the Caribbean. But, having wrapped himself and America in the U.S. flag (Bush supported the outlawing of flag burning), Bush succeeded not in asserting America's masculinity, but rather in raising the question of its sex and gender. "Dressing" the American body politic in the flag, Bush crossed over the signs/lines of masculinity and crossed out the certainty that the American body politic was male. Rather than replay Reagan's role as a simulated superhero who rescued America's sense of itself, Bush's invasion of Panama imitated what America most hoped to hide from itself—its own castration. America's encounter with its castrated self in Panama opened the American body politic up to reengendering and prepared it for its queering under President Clinton in the U.S.-led invasion of Haiti. But this was not before Bush led a "post-phallic" America—an America unable to assure itself not just the last word but a masculine voice in the Caribbean—to once again wonder who it was.

Male Hysteria or Nose Thumbing and Signposting

The hysteric...cannot assume his/her own discourse; everything is referred for validation to the "you." (Whitford, 1991: 35)

Failing in the field of simulation, Bush returned America to the field of referentality while simultaneously attempting to retain the rest of Reagan (as a simulated phallus) for the American body politic. A return to referentality for Bush meant that Bush's America asked "Who am I?" and it again referred this question to the Caribbean Sea/See/ Screen. The statement "I am" expresses subjectivity, whereas the questions "Who am I?" or "Am I?" denote hysteria. Hysteria has been defined as "a response in symptomatic form—that is, one made through a substitution of corporeal signifiers for unconscious impulses—to a sexual demand or urge that the subject cannot accommodate" (DiPiero, 1991: 104). Lack and excess are the two complementary motifs of hysteria. Hysteria appears as the excessive miming of masculinity (a miming that psychoanalytic discourse equates with subjectivity) that "stands in" for a lack of phallic power (inability to make meaning). In the case of female hysteria, this lack of phallic power follows from a lack of a penis.

Luce Irigaray reminds us that hysteria is not an exclusively female pathology (1985b: 46). Yet male hysteria takes a different form than female hysteria. Whereas female hysteria illustrates the coding of women as men, "what male hysteria shows us is not so much the coding of men as women, as the uncoding of men as men" (Kirby, 1988: 126). Male hysteria is the emasculation of men (uncoding of men as men) rather than the feminization of men (coding of men as women).

One expression of emasculation is the exposure of the phallus. Exposure combines excessive display with a lack of phallic power. Exposing the penis (excess) demonstrates the absence of phallic power (lack). Male hysterics, like female hysterics, excessively imitate or mime masculinity to compensate for a lack of phallic power; they do so not because they lack a penis, however, but because their penis is (over-)exposed.

Noriega's nose thumbing at Bush artfully combined excess and lack in the form of male hysteria. Referring to this gesture as the summary statement of why the United States invaded Panama, the White House adviser hinted at a pervasive hysterical backdrop. As they appear in the discourse concerning the invasion, both Noriega and Bush display hysterical symptoms.

To encounter Noriega is to encounter a symbolic excess of masculinity. Manuel Antonio Noriega's name—read as an acronym (MAN), as a proper name ([Man]uel), or as a nickname ([Man]ny) by an English-speaking subject such as Bush—attests to Noriega's manliness. So too do Noriega's possessions. Recounting the assets of

Noriega's personal fortune, Deputy Secretary of State Lawrence Eagleburger noted that Noriega has "Three large pleasure yachts, the Macho I, Macho II, and Macho III—now that's a lot of macho" (Eagleburger, 1989a: 3).

Bush's hysterical excess is displaced from his physical body to his geopolitical body, from George Bush the man onto George Bush the commander in chief of a posthegemonic/post-phallic/post-Reagan state. The military invasion of Panama marks the attempted masculine projection of Bush's stately authority not only into the international sphere but also into the territory of another domestic space, more specifically into the "Canal Zone"—a femininely engendered passageway (vagina) through which male/international subjects reach maturity. As in psychoanalytic discourse, it is the phallus that is the masculine projection of authority internationally and the feminine "hole"—the Panama Canal—that is its domestic and geopolitical underwriter.

In both of these cases, excess is tied to a lack of phallic power. For Noriega, phallic power is undercut by his lack of staying power. Shortly after the coup attempt of October 3, 1989, Noriega boasted that "Virility is proved by staying in [power]" *New York Times*, October 4, 1989; my insertion). Noriega's staying power was to last a brief time after this. Noriega's difficulty with staying in was that he was left with nothing to stay in. He had no domestic space, no nation-state, no canal in which he could express his phallic power. Noriega became a man without access to a canal—a hysterical male who, in this case, could be read as a man with a useless phallus, thanks to externally imposed celibacy.

Bush's lack manifested itself differently. Rather than having no domestic space(s) in which to project his authority, Bush projected a simulated hegemonic authority that was in decline. Debates about U.S. hegemony and the Reagan legacy of a United States transformed into the world's largest debtor state raised questions about America's phallic power. Did it exist under Bush as it did under Reagan—as simulated substitute or "reel" expression of American geopolitical and economic power? If so, was Bush man enough to sustain the imaginary image of America, or was he just a wimp?

Like Noriega's excess, Bush's lack plays on the thumb metaphor. While Noriega was thumbing his nose (waving his penis) at Bush, Bush was attempting to revisualize his stately thumb (America's penis coded as simulated hegemonic power). Touring Panama after the invasion, Representative Lee Hamilton observed that Panamanians would "come out and give us a thumbs up signal" (*Congressional Quarterly Weekly Report*, January 6, 1990: 43). To some, at least, the mission appeared to be a success.

Prior to the invasion, Bush's thumb did not speak so loudly in the region. To compensate for the impending impotence of a declining/fading image of American hegemony, a formal display of hegemonic power was offered by General Colin Powell, Chairman of the Joint Chiefs of Staff. Powell "is reported recently to have said that we have to put up a shingle outside our door saying 'superpower lives here...'" (*London Times*, December 22, 1989). Jacques Lacan argues that the phallus as the psychoanalytic standard of value functions as a signifier "only as veiled," but Powell's strategy of announcing the obvious contradicts the message he "posts." It is an act of exposure that "is the equivalent to announcing that the central postulate is in fact being called into question" (Irigaray, 1985a: 27). The announcement of hegemonic power unveils the phallus and displays the penis that cannot stand on its own. In this case, it announces that Bush cannot stand on his own without Reagan. This accounts for Senator Sam Nunn's insistence in the joint hearings on the invasion that American "[l]egitimacy...is going to depend on...reduced American visibility" (*Events in Panama*, 1989: 135).

Speculum of the Other Country

In her book *Speculum of the Other Woman*, Irigaray describes the relationship between the sexes in psychoanalytic discourse as "specularized." The word *speculum* refers to both an "instrument for dilating cavities of [the] human body for inspection" and a "mirror, usu. of polished metal" (*Oxford English Dictionary*; quoted in Moi, 1985: 130). Both the masculine and the feminine share aspects of the speculum. The masculine instrument or tool (the penis) penetrates the formless empty cavity (the vagina) of the feminine, and the feminine acts as a "faithful, polished mirror" that reproduces masculine subjectivity but not itself (Irigaray, 1985a: 136). The mirror (feminine) symbolized by the speculum depicts both the transformation of the mother into a ghost (specter) in the Lacanian mirror stage and the concavity of the mirror (speculum) that turns images upside down (ibid., 144).

Yet another meaning of speculum is a lens that focuses light on a hole. This understanding of speculum combines the masculine and feminine aspects of the term. Of the speculum, Irigaray writes, "It may, quite simply, be an instrument to dilate the lips, the orifices, the walls, so that the eye can penetrate the interior" (ibid.). She goes on to explain that man's eye is "understood as substitute for penis" (ibid., 145). It is by separating the vulva (lips) and penetrating the vagina with his penis (eye) that man sees his subjectivity reflected back at him in the concave mirror (woman). In Ronald Reagan's case, woman can be used not only as a mirror but as a screen onto which a simulated phallus is projected. The eye/phallus here both brings masculinity into a visual field and fools the eye as to the "reality" of how it sees its subjectivity (Debrix, 1999).

The masculine ability to penetrate and the feminine ability to reflect or simulate images correspond to a hierarchy of solids and fluids found in psychoanalytic theory. Visible forms (penis) are privileged over formless voids (vagina). As mentioned in the previous chapter, Irigaray's observation that gender is coded in terms of solids and fluids leads to her account of the potentially turbulent role the feminine may play in psychoanalytic discourse. The feminine as mirror or screen only reflects/projects masculine subjectivity if it is placid, unclouded, and fixed. When the feminine ceases to function as a reflective pool/simulating screen, masculine subjectivity is in crisis.

The Panama Canal

When described in terms of sex and gender, geopolitical bodies in international relations are most often coded as internally female/feminine and externally male/masculine. A sovereign nation-state, for example, is said to have a feminine domestic side and a masculine international side. "Domestic" refers to the private sphere of state relations that gives a particular state a unique national character. "International" refers to the projection of this domestic identity into the public sphere of relations among states. In international relations theory, as in Irigaray's account of psychoanalytic theory, these dual sex/gender codings are paired as opposites rather than queered or combined. The effect of this heterosexual pairing is to understand the feminine (domestic) as what makes the masculine (international) possible; for without a clearly identified domestic (feminine) sphere, the argument goes, a nation-state would have no voice to project into the international (masculine) sphere.

On a first reading, Panama and the United States can be described in these engendered terms. For each state, it is a domestic citizenry and territory (the feminine) that provides the basis for international authority (the masculine). When these heterosexually engendered geopolitical bodies are conjoined with the bodies of their respective heads of state, what are highlighted are the sources of hysteria for Noriega and Bush. What comes into focus is the particular geopolitical lack each leader compensates for through a discourse of excess.

Each leader in a different way lacks the feminine object that will affirm his masculine subjectivity. For Noriega, the feminine is a domestic space (a nation-state) that he can claim as his own so that Panama under his leadership will have a legitimate voice in international affairs. For Bush, the feminine object is an international space in which to project hegemonic authority. This space is also Panama. But in the Bush administration discourse, Panama does not compensate for Bush's lack of a domestic space; rather, Panama helps Bush compensate for his lack of the "vision thing," for it is in the Canal

Zone that U.S. hegemonic authority is reflected/screened. These two very different ways of understanding Panama as lack are combined in the discourse on the invasion through the Bush administration's attempt to project its authority internationally by withholding the feminine object from Noriega.

This feminine object shows up in the Bush administration discourse as both an anatomic and a geopolitical body. What these bodies have in common is they are victims of attempted rape by the Noriega administration. In his speech to the U.S. public outlining the justifications for intervention in Panama, Bush explicitly states that what all the fighting is about is sexual abuse. Panamanian "forces under his [Noriega's] command shot and killed an unarmed American serviceman; wounded another; arrested and brutally beat a third American serviceman; and then brutally interrogated his wife, threatening her with sexual abuse. That was enough" (Bush, 1990: 720).

The anatomic body of the American serviceperson's wife implies another body that, according to the Bush administration, Noriega sexually abuses. This feminine geopolitical body is the Panama Canal. Noriega's discourse inscribes the canal in similar terms to those used by Irigaray to describe how the feminine appears in psychoanalytic discourse. A few months before the invasion, Noriega commented: "Panama [is] like a mirror in which all of America . . . see themselves" (Noriega, 1989: 40–41). The locus of Panama's reflective/simulating power is the Panama Canal. State sovereignty is symbolized by the flagged ships of various nation-states floating in this man-made passageway that spawned a nation-state.

Noriega's rape of the canal seemed imminent to the Bush administration. The invasion occurred just eleven days before the administration of the canal was scheduled to be handed over to a Panamanian commission. Panamanian administrative control of the canal troubled the Bush administration because of Noriega's leadership style. In Bush administration discourse, Noriega signifies a disruptive force who threatens to stir the still waters of the canal. Discussing the invasion, General Kelly remarks about Noriega: "[H]e knows how to swim in that environment down there" (*Events in Panama*, 1989: 140). Another Bush administration official refers to Noriega's government and style of rule as "Noriega's Titanic" (Eagleburger, 1989b: 2).

A Bush administration official notes, "We must recognize . . . that Panama's ability to responsibly pursue its own interest—and hence the long-term future of the canal—cannot be assured in the context of political instability." The official stresses that democracy is "an essential element of political stability on the isthmus." The "firm" position of the Bush administration is that "securing the long-term future of democracy in Panama and of the canal" represents two elements that are "indissolubly linked. . . . Noriega's continuation in power is a threat. . . . And . . . it will be the canal's users who ultimately must face the burden of bearing the costs" (Kozak, 1989: 2).

Democracy is valued, then, for its stabilizing influence—for its ability to calm formless feminine fluids so they may heterosexually serve masculine purposes. Until a democratic environment could be established in Panama—until the Endara government could be seated—the United States had to retain administrative control of the canal. So long as Noriega governed Panama, he endangered the U.S. "broad national interest" of maintaining "a safe, efficient, and neutral Panama Canal" (ibid.). "Broad" in this context may refer to both the scope of U.S. interests and to a vernacular expression of the feminine component of U.S. interests.

Both interpretations are suggested by what became the epitome of the Bush presidency: "Read my lips." A symptomatic interpretation of this phrase replaces "lips" for "vulva." Bush's "lips," then, refer to the canal, "my" is his assertion of ownership of the canal, and "read" denotes the autistic character of the feminine (for, as Irigaray argues, the feminine lips cannot speak in a phallocentric discourse, although the lips simultaneously invoke language and the feminine). So long as his lips (the Panama Canal) can be read but cannot speak, Panamanian stability is ensured.

But, like General Powell's signposting, Bush's challenge to his audience ("Read my lips") is as disempowering as it is empowering. Bush's lips at once claim the Panama Canal as a reflective pool/simulating screen of U.S. hegemonic power and display the feminization of the U.S. president. Read as a sign of female reproductive ability more generally, Bush's lips silently announce that the president has egg on his face.

In the Bush administration discourse, a distinction is drawn between preserving Panamanian sovereignty and removing Noriega from power. What this suggests is that the Bush administration does not want to become the only user of the canal. Rather, the "neutrality" of the canal must be ensured so that the United States and Panama can be among the canal's users. The achievement of this goal entails separating the disruptive masculine subject (Noriega) from his feminine object (the canal). By denying Noriega his feminine object, the United States effectively denies Noriega's masculine subjectivity. And, as a head of state without a state, Noriega is no longer a threat to U.S. hegemony in the region. A joke by a senator at the joint congressional hearings on events in Panama explicitly links masculine subjectivity with the feminine object in a heterosexual combination. When a man testifying before the committee announced, "I was confirmed in June," a senator added, "No pun intended" (*Events in Panama,* 1989: 137). Read as the proper name of a woman rather than as a month, "June" signifies the body in which masculine subjectivity is achieved. It is not so much the pun as it is the pun's structure that is of interest here. Notice that it is the U.S. senator who substitutes the unconscious impulse (confirmation of male subjectivity in a female body) for the corporal signifier (June read as a woman's body), thereby revealing the hysterical subtext of the hearings.

Ironically, in the postinvasion discourse, "June" as a time/location serves as an embarrassing reminder that Bush's masculine subjectivity is unconfirmed. It was in June 1992 that Bush visited post–Noriega Panama, only to be greeted by "menacing stares and defiant thumbs-down gestures," as well as by a possible assassination attempt (*St. Croix Avis,* June 12, 1992: 35).

Speculum turned to spectacle when the United States invaded Panama to capture Noriega. And spectacle turned to farce while Noriega eluded the U.S. military. Even so, this moment of the invasion served the U.S. "broad" national interest. William Bennett, the president's director of national drug control policy, said of Noriega at this juncture, "He's not running drugs; he's not running Panama; he's just running" (*London Times*, December 21, 1989). The transformation of Noriega from solids to fluids guaranteed that he no longer posed a threat to the canal. Indeed, as the papal nuncio remarked, Noriega was politically castrated: "The entire nation thinks [Noriega is] a man endowed with powers he doesn't have. I found him a man who, without a pistol [penis], could be handled by anyone" (*Newsweek*, January 15, 1990; my insertion).

Specularized Policy

Military intervention joins the affirmation of state sovereignty with violence. In international relations theory, intervention is defined as the violation of one state's sovereignty by an uninvited intruder (Weber, 1995b). It is rape on an international scale. A panel at the 1991 American Political Science Association meetings conveys the masculine inscription of intervention and its relationship to a feminine object. The panel was called "Dilemma of Protracted [Specularized?] Intervention" (my insertion), and the primary titles of the papers were "Getting In," "Staying In," and "Getting Out."

Given this, the Bush administration's strategy of denying Noriega his feminine object (a nation-state and the canal) through the act of military intervention is consistent with the account of Bush as a hysterical male. If Bush embodies the United States during a refractory period/fading projection that signals the impending impotence of the United States (hegemonic/simulated decline), then the U.S. invasion of Panama exemplifies the excessive miming of masculinity. But this begs the question: Does a nearly impotent commander in chief have the capacity to "get in"? Put differently, is a declining hegemon able to project the image of its masculine subjectivity internationally through an act of military intervention?

The answer to these questions appears to be both yes and no. A U.S. military operation clearly took place in Panama. However, it replaced penetration with encirclement as its modus operandi. Instead of internationally projecting U.S. hegemonic power into the domestic affairs of Panama, the United States domesticated Panama. The U.S. discourse on Panama effectively subsumed Panamanian domestic affairs within the scope of U.S. domestic policy. Territorially, domestic/international boundaries did not change; discursively, however, Panama was left with no domestic sphere distinct from that of the United States. The U.S. strategy of encirclement made the more common intervention tactic of penetration unnecessary and therefore compensated for America's fading simulations. Thanks to this initial act of domestication, the invasion could be viewed as an internal act undertaken to consolidate one domestic space. U.S. images of phallic power in Panama were screened both for the United States (to restore itself as its own loved object) and *onto* itself (Panama as part of the United States).

Two factors make the U.S. domestication of Panamanian space possible. The first is historical. Panama's history as a sovereign nation-state cannot be separated from U.S. history. It was the U.S. desire for a canal in Central America in the early 1900s that led it to support a Panamanian claim of independence from Colombia. To this day, this initial act of genesis lingers in U.S.–Panamanian relations; for it is the United States that controls the vital circulatory systems of Panama — the Panama Canal and Panamanian currency (U.S. dollars).

Staged against a background of shared history is a second, more immediate factor — the U.S. discursive claim to Panama couched in terms of the "war on drugs." Although the Bush administration held that "This is a war as deadly and as dangerous as any fought with armies massed across boarders," its rhetoric on drugs erased any distinctions between what is domestic and what is international (Bush, 1989: 2). According to the administration, drug trafficking "is a worldwide problem" that "threatens the security of nations" (Eagleburger, 1989b: 2). "The drug issue knows no national borders" (Wolf, 1989: 2).

The administration's refusal of the domestic/international dichotomy makes Noriega's drug-related indictments by two Florida grand
juries less objectionable. Noriega is transformed from a head of state
to a common domestic criminal. "The story these indictments tell is
simple and chilling. It is the story of that same shameless excess in
the criminal field that we have already seen in the political field" (Eagleburger, 1989a: 6). Bringing Noriega to justice means bringing Noriega to trial in the United States. The community of judgment in this
case was a jury composed of U.S. citizens. "Justice" here refers to
U.S. domestic justice and not international justice.

The Bush administration discourse on the invasion of Panama
always finds a point of reference, and this point is the refigured United
States that surrounds Panama. Unlike the U.S. intervention of Grenada
in 1983, the United States did not direct its justification for intervention in Panama to some simulated international community. No organization analogous to the Organization of Eastern Caribbean States
was created so that it could "ask" for U.S. military assistance. A regional or international request for intervention was unnecessary because the U.S. invasion of Panama was an internal matter. Only the
U.S. citizenry needed to be "consulted" and, in the event of a military
action, offered an explanation. "Operation Just Cause," the administration's code name for the invasion, was just by U.S. domestic standards and was justified to the U.S. public. In this sense, the invasion
discourse was more than referential. It was self-referential, which is
one aspect of simulation.

The U.S. invasion of Panama abides by a specularized logic both
because it transforms a traditional account of intervention into its
negative image and because the traditional locations of domestic and
international policy appear upside down in the concave mirror/screen
of Panama. With respect to intervention, the Bush administration's
domestication of Panama reinscribes the meaning of intervention in
this case. President Bush asks, "[W]hat, in God's name, would we . . .
call the international drug trade — and those who aid it and abet it —

but intervention in our internal affairs?" (Bush, 1989: 2). This notion is expanded upon by Eagleburger:

> There are times when good principles force us to defend bad men. Some argue that this is the case with Noriega and Panama. They argue as if the principle of nonintervention requires us to accept whatever Noriega does.
>
> But nonintervention was never meant to protect individual criminals. It was never meant to promote intervention by drug traffickers in our societies against our families and children. It was never meant to prevent peaceful and diplomatic action by sovereign states in support of democracy. And it was never meant to leave the criminals free to savage the good and the good powerless to react. (Eagleburger, 1989a: 6)

Additionally, the strategy of encirclement specularizes the logic of the invasion by transposing domestic and international policy. The U.S. war on drugs encircles Noriega in a threefold sense: first by the domestication of Panamanian policy, second by surrounding the Vatican embassy with rock-and-roll music, and third by encapsulating Noriega in a U.S. prison cell. Manuel Noriega—the head of state of an independent sovereign nation—became U.S. federal prisoner no. 41586. Looking at the discourse of the U.S. invasion of Panama, one finds foreign policy located in U.S. domestic space (Noriega in a U.S. prison) and domestic policy located in a foreign space (the U.S. war on drugs fought in Panama).

This State Which Is Not One

In her book *this sex which is not one*, Luce Irigaray described feminine sexuality as not one sex but as more than one. It is this surplus sexuality that disrupts phallocentric economies of desire. For Irigaray, surplus sexuality is not the same thing as hysterical excess because surplus sexuality is a *quality* of the feminine sex. Yet, when practiced, what Irigaray codes as a quality—surplus sexuality—I suggest recodes any sexual subject as feminine. Moving from an essential quality to a sexually transformative practice not only potentially dismantles phallocentric economies of desire (as Irigaray argues) but also (as I will argue) disrupts phallocentric economies of heterosexuality.

Surplus sexuality emerges in the U.S. invasion of Panama to disrupt U.S. projections of itself as hegemonically masculine—that is, as male, as phallic, and as straight. In this invasion, the American body politic is both hystericized and feminized. Male hysteria refers to the uncoding of men as men (emasculation or phallic loss) and feminization refers to the coding of men as women (grafting feminine surplus sexuality onto a male body). That Noriega and Bush lack phallic power and compensate for this lack with the excessive miming of masculinity indicates male hysteria. In their moments of excess, the bodies of Noriega and Bush are also femininely engendered. Recall, for example, Noriega's transformation from solids to fluids and Bush's display of female reproductive organs on his face. Furthermore, the name "Bush" announces the location of female genitalia. By claiming the Canal Zone as part of the American body politic, Bush grafted these Panamanian lips onto the U.S. body, foreshadowing the transsexualizing of this body under President Clinton. The most critical moment of feminization in the invasion discourse pertains to the Bush administration's strategy of encirclement. This move deconstructs masculine standards of "international" and "intervention" and begins to queer the American body politic.

For Bush and the United States, hysteria or the crisis in subjectivity is brought about by the decline of America's simulated hegemony. The Panama Canal functions in Bush's discourse as the reflective pool/screen that can mirror/project U.S. hegemonic subjectivity. Because the U.S. invasion of Panama secured the stability of the canal, one might conclude that the reflective/simulating function of the canal, and therefore U.S. hegemonic subjectivity, are rescued.

This conclusion overlooks the feminization of Bush and the United States—the surplus sexuality that the Bush administration performatively grafted onto the American body politic during the invasion of Panama. It neglects the implications of an intervention strategy based on encirclement rather than penetration. As noted earlier, intervention in international relations theory is rape on an international scale. Rape commonly refers to an act committed by a male on a female or a male. Considered from a psychoanalytic perspective, the U.S. invasion of Panama might be said to include two different scenarios of rape—the first by a woman on a man and the second by a male transvestite on a woman. These unusual sex/gender pairings of rape—by female to male and by male transvestite to female—are suggested by penis envy (women presumably wanting to possess a penis) and the threat of castration (men fearing the loss of the function of their penis) as they appear in psychoanalytic discourse.

The first rape scenario—female on male—symbolizes the threat of castration. In psychoanalytic discourse, the threat of castration is not reserved for the Father, who is located on the side of the Law and the phallus. The woman too may pose this threat to a man, only differently. Whereas the Father's threat is to cut off his son's genitals, the woman's threat—owing to her presumed penis envy—is to refuse to relinquish the penis that has penetrated her. Should the woman whose body encircles the penis refuse to surrender it, the male would experience a similar sense of loss as he would if he were actually castrated. Encirclement and entrapment, then, are modalities of female rape of a male.

In the discourse of the U.S. invasion of Panama, it is the feminized Panama Canal that threatens to encircle and symbolically castrate Noriega and Bush. Noriega never experiences this form of castration because the Bush administration denies him access to the canal and thus symbolically castrates him first. Bush also avoids castration by the canal—not because he is denied access to it but because, even given access, he is incapable of penetration. Bush, like the American body politic, is already symbolically castrated. In this regard, the canal's threat of castration to Bush serves as an embarrassing reminder of

America's lack of phallic power. For both Noriega and Bush, the threat of castration posed by the Panama Canal is never anything more than a threat.

Even though it is not actualized, this first rape scenario is important because it acts as an interpretive guide for the second rape scenario—by a male transvestite on a female. A male transvestite is a man acting and/or appearing as a woman. Although this transvestite is anatomically male, his actions and dress are those of a female. The transvestite is both emasculated (a man uncoded as a man) and feminized (a man recoded as a woman).

In the U.S. invasion of Panama, the transvestite is Bush acting on behalf of the American body politic and the female is the Panama Canal. Bush is a transvestite in international politics not only because he has wrapped himself in America's "dress" red, white, and blue, but also because, in the presumably masculine arena of international politics, his actions as commander in chief are feminine. The U.S. invasion of Panama is a feminine act because it is carried out via a strategy of encirclement. This act of encirclement takes on interesting implications when examined psychoanalytically. As noted earlier, encirclement may be interpreted both as the threat of castration and as female rape. When encirclement as rape occurs to a female (the Panama Canal), the threat of castration is canceled out because the female in psychoanalytic discourse is already castrated. The focus, then, is on female rape.

This act of female rape by Bush has two effects. First, it suggests that in the international arena where states project their masculine authority, the masculinely engendered United States is reengendered as feminine. The move from penetration to encirclement marks the uncoding of man as man as well as the recoding of man as woman. This first effect is emphasized by the second effect: rather than miming masculinity directly (hysteria), Bush's miming of masculinity is once removed. What Bush mimes is female rape, specifically the American body politics threatened rape or encirclement by the Panama Canal. Thanks to the declining hegemon's inability to project its phallic power

into international politics, Bush is only able to mime the American
body politic's castration through the female model of rape. The U.S.
invasion of Panama reminds Bush that he and his state have already
been effectively castrated because they are seemingly impotent. They
have already been rewritten as feminine. Because this reinscription of
man as woman occurs in what should be the international sphere reserved for actions by male subjects, Bush and the American body
politic appear as transvestites rather than as a women. Marked as
a transvestite in international politics, the American body politic is
queered. This body — similar to the body of Castro's Cuba — appears
in the invasion discourse as a third term, as the neither/nor (neither
masculine nor feminine). The American body politic performs its surplus sexuality as a queered/nonnormalized subject.

Two final implications of the invasion are suggested by this reading. If, as Freud and Lacan argue, it is through the castration complex that subjects enter the symbolic order and become "civilized,"
then the fading hegemon's confrontation with his own castration marks
the end of one symbolic order and the beginning of a new order. During
the invasion, the American body politic confronted its own castration
that it then mimed through its intervention strategy of encirclement.
This encounter with its castration and feminization in international
politics led the United States and Bush to reinscribe the symbolic order
in terms that could accommodate the refigured American body. In
this "New World Order," two quite different models of "civilization"
or "meaning" are at work. For Panama, the terms of the old international order are still meaningful. Although Noriega has been effectively castrated by the United States, Panama without Noriega appears
in this order as simply "immature." It can reach maturity under the
terms of the "old" world order when it receives possession of the Canal
Zone at the turn of the century. The United States, in contrast, is mature but seemingly impotent. In its old age, it must go through a re-
civilizing process into a "New World Order" in which its international interactions will be expressed by the body of a man acting as a
woman. This post-Reagan, posthegemonic state is also a "post-phallic"

state because it is no longer able to sustain its projected phallic simulations. Bush's America cannot stand on its own. As compensation, it grafts female modalities of action onto the male American body.

The result is a mixing of sexual bodies (male and female) and gender codings (masculine and feminine) in ways that threaten to confound heterosexual codings of geopolitical bodies. Intervention may still be rape and the bodies that perform that rape may still be male, but the performance of the rape mimes the female threat of castration. Given this and given that intervention practices are only meaningful in the international arena, the old dichotomy of domestic = feminine/ international = masculine does not refer to America's posthegemonic, "post-phallic" body. The U.S. invasion of Panama deconstructs the terms *masculine* and *international* in this dichotomy, for contained in the masculine, international realm are feminine processes of intervention. Similar to how Irigaray described women in psychoanalytic discourse, the American body politic under Bush is both a state and a sex which is not one. It is a lesser, impaired state because it lacks the ability to project phallic power internationally. Described in terms of sex, it is a hysterical man. Furthermore, this body is not just one but more than one. Its surplus again may be described in gendered terms. Internationally (or in what traditionally is regarded as the international realm), it is a transvestite. It is a cross-dressed man who abides by female modes of conduct. America's surplus sexuality in the Panama invasion does not reinforce the distinction between sexes and genders as it does in Irigaray's discourse. Instead, it begins to queer them — to mix them in boundary-crossing ways that not so much remark as *un*mark sexual subjectivity and (in this case) the sex and gender of U.S. hegemony.

Taking transvestite subjectivity into account leads to a rethinking of sexual difference because transvestites — subjects who combine male and female terms — disrupt the logic whereby sexuality can be managed with dichotomies. This is so as much for some theories of psychoanalysis (those of Freud and Lacan, for example) as it is for theories of international relations.

Transvestite transgressions have the effect of destabilizing the subjectivity of singularly sexed bodies — both diplomatic and territorial. Because the United States and its president do not represent stable, single-sexed subjects, they signify an erasure rather than a reinscription of gender dichotomies. It is a misreading to continue to describe these bodies as either males acting as women or women miming the actions of men because, in a "post-phallic" world order, the male/female and masculine/feminine dichotomies break down. Transvestite subjectivity embodied in a state or a statesperson focuses attention on the artificial and arbitrary distinction between that which is male and that which is female and between that which is domestic and that which is international.

Transvestite subjectivity suggests another series of possible (un)inscriptions of gender that can be found in diplomatic practice. It is not long before the American body politic realizes their phallic potential and deploys them. Combining mixed sex and gender terms, it is as a seemingly self-aware transvestite/transsexual that President Bill Clinton leads the American body politic in the "intervasion" of Haiti.

6. MASQUERADING AMERICA AND THE U.S. "INTERVASION" OF HAITI

Rephallusization can come in the most unlikely disguises. During the first term of the Clinton administration, the American body politic seemed to regain its regional phallus—and the sense of hegemonic identity that comes with it—by faking it. But the Clinton administration's move was not to fake having the phallus but to fake *not* having the phallus. Following President Bush's example of wrapping the American body politic in the American flag, this administration did the same. But the effect was not as it had been in Bush's case—to confront a transvestized American body politic with its symbolic castration. Instead, for the Clinton administration the effect was to seemingly assert a transvestite/transsexualized subjectivity that keep international others guessing as to America's phallic endowments. Did the American body politic have the phallus? If so, was it "real" or was it "fake"? And could the perception of America's phallic lack since its confrontation with Castro's Cuba have been just a mistake?

President Clinton's deliberate faking of phallic lack is familiar enough. It was his strategy in the Clinton–Monica Lewinsky sex scandal—a scandal in which "the American president's sex organ seems to have become the center of the universe" (former French minister of culture Jack lang; *International Herald Tribune,* Bologna, August 18, 1998: 1–3). More generally, Clinton's deliberate faking of phallic lack as a strategy for rephallusizing the American body politic was consistent with the central motif of his administration's first term: mixing. Clinton's presidential body was the location for a mixing of gender, sex, and sexuality. Clinton's appointment of his wife Hillary Rodham Clinton to head up a commission on health care sent out mixed signals about the president's gender. Was he masculine enough to run the country? Was he dominated by a wife he could not keep to the role as a more conservatively defined "traditional" first lady? Were Clinton's lacks so severe that he needed a woman—his wife (and several others)—to compensate for his inadequacies and make him appear to be masculine? Or was Clinton so secure in his masculinity that he was not threatened by his policy-competent lawyer partner?

Sexually, President Clinton's body was mixed up with that of former President Jimmy Carter. This is not as surprising as it may at first appear because Clinton's presidential body has long been a site of mixing with the figures of other political personae. Clinton was identified with President Kennedy during his campaign and in the first months of his presidency. After Clinton's second-term accident in which he tore ligaments in his knee, he appeared first as the figure of Franklin Delano Roosevelt in a wheelchair and later slipped into the character of Winston Churchill with his cane. But Clinton's mixing with President Carter—at least through his first term—was the most striking.

This mixing began with Clinton's appointment of former Carter administration officials—such as Carter's former undersecretary of state, Warren Christopher, as secretary of state—and was exaggerated by the regular foreign-policy roles Carter himself received during Clinton's first term. Eventually, Clinton's presidential body was crossed over and crossed out by the presidential body of Carter, a body often read as feminine. On its own, Clinton's sexual body signifies sexual harassment of women, while Carter's body signifies sexual purity, even if, as the former president admitted to *Playboy* magazine, he had "committed adultery in my heart." Crossing the sexual identities of presidential bodies also crosses the body of the American politic. Attired in America's "dress" red, white, and blue (a legacy from the Bush administration), this body is already cross-dressed. Adding to the American body the mixed sexual qualities of these crossed presidents refigures the sexuality of the American body politic as both hyperaggressive and hyperrepressed, the two stereotypical expressions of extreme male and extreme female sexual behavior. This American body politic is on the verge of being transsexed and seems ready for all manner of rephallusization, however queer it might happen to be.

It is a queer phallus, neither real nor fake, that the American body politic harnesses to itself during the 1994 U.S.-led intervention into Haiti. Further mixing the presidential bodies of Clinton and Carter, President Clinton returned the former president center stage as informal mediator between the U.S. and the de facto government of General Raoul Cédras, which the United States hoped to replace with the democratically elected government of Father Jean-Bertrand Aristide. In so doing, he symbolically queered the American body politic in a Caribbean context.

In keeping with the mixing motif, the Clinton administration insisted that the U.S.-led invasion of Haiti never happened. U.S. forces landed in Haiti in September 1994. The Cédras government relinquished power to the Aristide government. United Nations forces (of which approximately half were estimated to be U.S. forces) "replaced" the U.S. forces and remained in Haiti until the 1996 transfer of presidential power. Casualties were incurred on all sides. But, as President Clinton told the American people in a televised address on September 18, an invasion of Haiti was averted. What took its place, the administration suggested some days later, was an "incursion" or an "occupation," or even an "intervasion" (*Newsweek*, October 3, 1994: 32). It was, as Admiral Paul David Miller, commander in chief of the U.S. Atlantic Command, described it, "a tailored force." He elaborated:

> [W]e had two options, right? I phrased one called "kick in the door," and the other phrase is "a soft landing." . . . But with the President Carter/Senator Nunn/Colin Powell agreement, we sort of went in between those two bookends, is how I characterized it. . . . We had a tailored force, tailored

for that aspect of the mission; it was the right force at the right time. (Defense Department regular briefing, October 20, 1994; Federal News Service, 1994: 3)

This move from an invasion force to a differently tailored force highlights both the transvestite terms in which the United States described the invasion and one of the truisms of U.S. foreign policy toward Haiti — what you see is not necessarily what you get. Although this has been increasingly apparent in U.S. policy toward the Caribbean in the 1980s and 1990s, the Haiti intervasion moves U.S. foreign policy beyond (in)effective simulation to a different kind of manipulation of appearances — dissimulation (Weber, 1995a). Dissimulation, like simulation, is a fooling of the eye. But, unlike simulation, dissimulation does not fool the eye by projecting images that are more real than the real itself. Instead, dissimulation is a strategy of projecting images of the fake to celebrate rather than conceal the apparent absence of the real. What the Haiti intervention unveils (or maybe veils) is a dissimulated U.S. foreign-policy strategy, presidential masquerade.

Phallic Avowal and Disavowal

"Who Has the Phallus?"
"I Thought *You* Had the Phallus."
"Give Me Back That Phallus." (Bérubé and Graff, 1994)

Mary Ann Doane argues, "To masquerade is to manufacture a lack in the form of a certain distance between oneself and one's image" (1991: 26). It is a strategy whereby something is added (clothes or a demeanor, for example) not to conceal a lack, but rather to create the appearance of one. In the U.S. invasion of Panama, lack appeared as a lack of phallic power that was exhibited symptomatically through male hysteria. Although the meaning of lack remains the same in this chapter, its function differs. Male hysteria equates a lack of phallic power with an inability to make meaning. Meaning cannot be made because the phallus is exposed. Masquerade, in contrast, equates a lack of phallic power with a *reluctance* to make meaning. This reluctance to make meaning is performed by "pretending" not to possess that which would allow one to make meaning, the phallus. As Doane suggests, "masquerade is anti-hysterical for it works to effect a separation between the cause of desire and oneself" (ibid.). Whereas the hysteric asks "Am I?" the masquerading subject performatively replies "I am without desire."

"Pretending" not to possess the phallus is, of course, always a double pretending because, as Jacques Lacan reminds us (Lacan, 1985), no one actually can "be" or "have" the phallus. As Judith Butler explains, " 'Being' the Phallus and 'having' the Phallus denote divergent sexual positions, or nonpositions (impossible positions, really), within language. To 'be' the Phallus is to be the 'signifier' of the desire of the Other and *to appear* as this signifier" (Butler, 1990: 44). "Women are said to 'be' the Phallus in the sense that they maintain the power to reflect or represent the 'reality' of the self-grounding postures of the masculine subject.... Hence, 'being' the Phallus is always a 'being for' a masculine subject who seeks to reconfirm and augment his identity through the recognition of that 'being for' " (ibid., 45). In its quest for hegemonic identity, the United States needed the feminized Caribbean Sea/See/Screen to "be" the phallus for it.

"On the other hand," writes Butler,

> men are said to "have" the Phallus, yet never to "be" it, in the sense that the penis is not equivalent to the Law and can never fully symbolize that Law. Hence, there is a necessary or presuppositional impossibility to any effort to occupy the position of "having" the Phallus, with the consequence that both positions of "having" and "being" are, in Lacan's terms, finally to be understood as comedic failures that are nevertheless compelled to articulate and enact these repeated impossibilities. (Ibid., 46)

Although it is impossible to "be" or to "have" the phallus, it is not impossible to "appear" (not) to be or (not) to have the phallus. This is the very sense of pretending, the "seems to" space in a Lacanian economy of desire. It is the space of masquerade.

Discussions of masquerade in the psychoanalytic literature originated with and continue to focus primarily on female masquerade.

Female masquerade involves seeming not to have a will to the phallus by acting excessively feminine. An excess of "being" the phallus covers for a will to "have" the phallus. In this sense, "Womanliness therefore could be assumed and worn as a mask, both to hide the possession of masculinity and to avert the reprisals expected if she was found to possess it" (Riviere, 1929: 306).

Like female masquerade, male masquerade is also a strategy undertaken "to avert the reprisals expected if [he] was found to possess [the phallus]" (ibid.). Male masquerade involves a seeming not to possess that which one is presumed to possess, the phallus. It is a disavowal of the phallus that is also a disavowal of the penis, an adding on of clothes or a demeanor in order to appear to lack the phallus (and penis) and the ability to make meaning that might come from its possession.

This substituting of "seeming not to have" the phallus for "having" the phallus is one space of the male transvestite, "who . . . is careful to hide the wherewithal to dumbfound his neighbor" (Millot, 1990: 12). "Dumbfounding one's neighbor" as to one's lack of the phallus is a strategy undertaken not for its own sake but, as Marjorie Garber suggests, as a way of "protecting against the threat of loss" of the phallus (1992: 356). Writes Garber, "The theatrical transvestite literalizes the anxiety of phallic loss. The overdetermination of phallic jokes, verbal and visual, that often accompany transvestism onstage, is a manifestation of exactly this strategy of reassurance for anxiety through artifactual overcompensation" (ibid., 256). Emily Apter puts it differently, remarking that male transvestism "implicitly reinforce[s] the security of being male" (1991: 93). Precisely because the sartorial subject is dressed in women's clothes, the viewer's attention is drawn to the fact that he is male, has the penis, and could "have" the phallus.

The strategy of male masquerade serves two purposes. In its performance of phallic disavowal, it protects the male subject from the threat of castration (because he "seems to" already have been castrated), all the while underscoring that he is in possession of the penis and could possibly wield phallic power. Male masquerade is literally a strategy that enables the subject to have it both ways.

The United States was confident that it possessed the phallus in U.S.–Caribbean relations until its encounter with the Castro regime. Since that time, U.S.–Caribbean policy has consisted of a series of displacements of castration or castration anxiety, often through a strategy of simulating phallic power (as the United States did in the Grenada invasion and attempted but failed to do in the Panama invasion).

In a post–Cold War era, one would expect that the U.S. castration complex would have been overcome, especially with respect to the Caribbean. The United States emerged from the Cold War as the sole superpower in international affairs. Its position as leader of the New World Order, while challenged, was undeniable. U.S. principles became even more internationalized, for example, as the United States now garnered the forces of the United Nations without Soviet opposition to lead a victorious multinational force during the Persian Gulf War. President Bush claimed to have fought and won the Vietnam War, this time in the Persian Gulf, while candidate Clinton had told the American electorate, "If I win, it will finally close the book on Vietnam" (*Time*, November 16, 1992: 50). Whether through simulated victory in the Gulf or through generational rejuvenation, the "Vietnam syndrome" no longer seemed to plague Americans. Surely, from Clinton's election on — if not earlier — the United States possessed undisputed powers to make international meaning. America's perceived phallic lack must have been just a mistake.

Yet U.S. foreign policy toward the Caribbean did not exhibit these same characteristics. The Persian Gulf War may have been another dose of the medicine that promised to cure a nation ailing from the legacy of Vietnam, but its victory did not have the same affect for the United States in the Caribbean. The Bush administration's invasion of Panama that preceded the Persian Gulf War attempted to conceal a U.S. lack of phallic power in the Caribbean (and internationally); however, this failed simulation of U.S. phallic power only drew greater attention to U.S. lack. Although the Persian Gulf War redressed/reveiled this lack internationally, it did not calm the turbulent forces in the Caribbean. Without regional hegemony, American global hegemony would always be in doubt. This post–Cold War American body politic had to find a way to recover from its encounter with Castro's Cuba and reclaim its hegemonic identity in the Caribbean Sea/See/Screen without resorting to the sort of all-out use of force it did to win the "Vietnam War" in the Gulf.

Restored with a sense of youthful virility internationally, how could the United States act in its "own backyard" without both seeming to be a bully and risking future castration of the working phallus it had just presumably regained? It was precisely the unconscious desire to escape from castration anxiety that led the Clinton administration to disavow "its" phallus and become reluctant to undertake meaningful actions in its foreign policy. As President Clinton said in a speech before the United Nations General Assembly just after the Haiti intervention, "The problem is deciding when we must respond [to crises], and how we shall overcome our reluctance" (Federal News Service, September 26, 1994: 5). How the United States overcame its reluctance in the U.S.-led intervasion of Haiti was to appropriate drag as a foreign-policy strategy.

Who Was That Masked Man?

> Our allies feel that we've neglected them.... Under this administration we've also had an inclination to...keep separate the European countries, thinking that if they are separate, then we can dominate them and proceed with our secret, Lone Ranger-type diplomatic efforts. (Governor Jimmy Carter criticizing the foreign policy of the Ford administration in the Carter–Ford presidential debates [Kraus, 1979: 486])

> I have also not had the United States be the Lone Ranger. We had the U.N. come in here. (President Bill Clinton, speaking of the Haiti intervention [wire service interview; Federal News Service, September 14, 1994: 11]).

The U.S. foreign-policy strategy toward Haiti called on a masked man. Just who this masked man was—Bill Clinton, Jimmy Carter, or some composite of presidents and unofficial diplomats—was presented less clearly in U.S. foreign-policy discourse than who he was not and what he appeared not to have. He was no "Lone Ranger." And whoever he was, he appeared not to "have" the phallus.

The insistence of President Clinton that the United States was no Lone Ranger in the Haiti intervasion is important. It not only introduces the notion of masquerade into U.S. foreign policy, but it also points to *how* the mask was worn to create lack. As Clinton himself suggests, the construction of lack involved the U.S. relationship to the United Nations.

The intervasion into Haiti was not a U.S. mission. It was a United Nations mission led by the United States. This situation in and of itself is not unique. Under the Bush administration, for example, the United States led United Nations coalition forces during the Persian Gulf War. But how the United States positioned itself in relation to the United Nations was different in the Persian Gulf War than it was in the Haiti intervasion. In the case of the Persian Gulf War, President Bush asked for and received U.S. congressional support for the pending U.S. role in the war. Although the United States pushed its "line in the sand" political deadline for Iraqi withdrawal from Kuwait through the United Nations Security Council, it did not rely on United Nations authorization for its activities in the Gulf. Its authorization came from the U.S. Congress, which could trace the legitimacy for this move back to an enthusiastic U.S. public. The United Nations was simply an international organization through which U.S. domestic authorization was channeled and that itself could once again "stand in" for U.S. phallic rigidity (Debrix, 1999).

The United States–United Nations relationship during the Haiti affair was altogether different. Repeatedly, the Clinton administration pointed out that it was Resolution 940 of the United Nations Security Council, not the U.S. Congress, that provided the Clinton administration with authorization to invade Haiti. In his September 15, 1994, speech explaining the necessity of the Haiti invasion, Clinton told the American people that "the United Nations Security Council approved a resolution that authorizes the use of all necessary means, including force, to remove the Haitian dictators from power and restore demo-cratic government" (Federal News Service, 1994: 4).

President Clinton made it clear in a press conference that although he would welcome congressional support for the Haiti invasion, "the action of the United Nations should not be interpreted as an approval by Congress" (White House news conference; Federal News Service, August 3, 1994: 7). The administration also noted in comments to the media that it was aware of how unpopular the Haiti invasion was with the American people and made no claim that it was a groundswell of public support that authorized the administration's plans. As the president put it on September 14, "I realize it [the invasion] is unpop-ular. I know the timing is unpopular; I know the whole thing is un-popular. But I believe it is the right thing" (Federal News Service, 1994: 6).

United Nations authorization of the U.S.-led invasion was in-strumental in both accentuating U.S. lack and creating additional U.S. lack. The need for United Nations authorization itself stemmed from a U.S. lack—specifically, of public and congressional support for the invasion, as well as an assumed "lack of will" on the part of the United States to undertake meaningful foreign-policy action on its own. This was suggested by President Clinton in his September 15 address: "[T]he United States has agreed to lead a multinational force to carry out *the will of the United Nations*" (ibid., 4; my emphasis).

Already wrapped in the American flag, the American body politic sought to "accessorize" its internal lack (of domestic support and will to invade) by wearing the emblem of international lack itself—the United Nations. The United Nations is emblematic of lack in this situation because it cannot make war—declared or undeclared. This is a right reserved for individual, sovereign nation-states. Although the United Nations has supported its member states' war-making ac-tivities (as it did in the Gulf) and "humanitarian interventions" (such as Somalia), the United Nations itself has no authority to make war or to provide one of its member states with such authority. Instead,

United Nations support traditionally has been given to such activities in the name of peace — to oppose Iraqi aggression in Kuwait, to assist the civilian victims of Somalia's civil war, and to broker a peace in the former Yugoslavia, for example. It would be difficult to argue that United Nations Declaration 940, which "authorized" all necessary means to remove the Cédras de facto government from power, was anything but a veil for U.S. regional interests, interests the United States refused to pursue except while covered by the United Nations.

United Nations authorization of U.S. actions in Haiti allowed the United States to decorate its regional effort with flags of many nations. The multinational intervention force that the United States led in the Haiti intervasion included such unlikely participants as Poland, Israel, Jordan, and Bangladesh. As the list of member states in this force grew to more than thirty, it appeared less and less like a "genuine" response by the international community to the Haiti situation and more and more like the artificial, dissimulated cover for U.S. regional activity that it was. As William Safire commented in a *New York Times* essay, "With his ludicrous enlistment of cooks and bottle washers from every country on our foreign-aid list, Mr. Clinton fooled nobody but himself about this being an international operation. To pretend it is not our show to solve our refugee problem invites smirks around the world" (September 19, 1994).

What drew the most attention to the false appearance of the multinational force was that it was unprecedented for the United States to get extraregional support to carry out foreign-policy activities in its own "backyard" that it deemed to be in its national interest. Certainly, the United States had had regional participation in its Caribbean invasions in the past. Recall, for example, how the Organization of Eastern Caribbean States "requested" a U.S. invasion of Grenada and joined forces with the United States during this invasion. Moreover, it has been customary for the United States to request approval for its regional activities both from the Organization of American States and from the United Nations (approval that more often than not has been withheld). But never before had there been extraregional military participation in a U.S.-led regional intervention, nor had United Nations approval of a U.S. mission been required. This seemed to change with the Haiti invasion. Remarked President Clinton, "the United States must not be in a position to walk away from a situation like this in our backyard, while we expect others to lead the way in their backyard as long as the United Nations has approved of an operation" (wire service interview; Federal News Service, September 14, 1994: 4). Clinton's statement makes United Nations approval conditional for all nation-states, including the United States, hoping to act in their spheres of influence.

If all of this amounts to a lack of desire on the part of the United States to invade Haiti, why did an intervasion occur at all? Was it, as the Joint Chiefs of Staff joked in reference to "Operation Just Cause" in Panama, "Operation Just Because?" (*Newsweek*, October 3, 1994). Or was it, as the Clinton administration admitted, ultimately an issue of regional and international credibility (televised address; Federal News Service, September 15, 1994: 1)? And if so, how could a strategy of constructing a lack on the part of the United States possibly restore U.S. credibility?

There are a number of ways in which lack can be constructed in an intervention scenario. What the Clinton administration did was create a specific type of lack. Its apparent unwillingness (or at least reluctance) to make meaning in foreign policy was a strategy that protected the United States both from the charge of being a regional bully and from the threat of (future?) castration. Should the United States have refused to become involved in the Haitian intervasion, it would have left unredressed a lack of phallic power that was its regional legacy from the recent Panama invasion and the more menacing memory of its encounter with Castro's Cuba. Masquerade was an empowering strategy for the United States, a strategy that enabled it to escape the charge of regional impotence and sidestep the charge of regional bully.

Although the United States appeared not to "have" the phallus in its foreign policy toward Haiti, it was also careful not to appear to "be" the phallus for Haiti. Clinton's declaration that the United States was no Lone Ranger in the Haiti intervention can be read as both a construction of a particular type of lack (appearing not to "have" the phallus) and an attempted avoidance of any overt homoerotic subtext ("being" the phallus for another subject, maybe Tonto?). This does not mean that the American body politic was not queered in its intervasion of Haiti, nor that this queering was not unconsciously embraced as a rephallusizing strategy by the Clinton administration. Instead, it implies that as a queered subject, the American body politic was careful to remain crossed—as neither male nor female, neither masculine nor feminine. In this sense, the intervasion marks a move beyond rape, beyond sex, and beyond desire in U.S. foreign-policy discourse.

This can be illustrated by contrasting the Haiti intervention with the Panama invasion. Unlike the U.S. invasion of Panama (in which the United States "raped" Panama as a woman would rape a man), the U.S. intervention into Haiti disavowed "forced entry" altogether. It took place in a "permissive environment" (White House regular briefing; Federal News Service, September 8, 1994) in which violence and sex were exchanged for a "soft landing" and a disavowal of desire. No cast of diplomatic characters could have been better suited to negotiate this unforced entry than former President Jimmy Carter, former chairperson of the Joint Chiefs of Staff General Colin Powell, and chairperson of the Senate Armed Services Committee Sam Nunn.

A Diplomatic Parade of Unmarked Transvestites

[T]he quality of crossing—which is fundamentally related to other kinds of boundary-crossing in their performances— can be more powerful and seductive than explicit "female impersonation," which is often designed to confront, scandalize, titillate, or shock. (Garber, 1992: 354)

In her book *Vested Interests: Cross-Dressing and Cultural Anxiety,* Marjorie Garber introduces the figure of the "unmarked transvestite"—a figure who both challenges the possibility of representation and draws attention to "an *unconscious* of transvestism, for transvestism as a language that can be read, and double-read, like a dream, a fantasy, or a slip of the tongue" (ibid.; emphasis in original). She continues, "For while it is easy to speak of the power of transvestite display in figures like David Bowie, Boy George, and Annie Lennox, these overt cross-dressers, 'marked transvestites,' may in fact merely literalize something that is more powerful when masked or veiled—that is, when it remains unconscious" (ibid., 356). Garber confines her analysis to the domain of theater "to explore the possibility that some entertainers who do not overtly claim to be 'female impersonators,' for example, may in fact signal their cross-gender identities onstage" (ibid., 354).

I transfer Garber's analysis of the theatrical stage to the diplomatic stage, where Jimmy Carter, Colin Powell, and Sam Nunn as the diplomatic team representing U.S. foreign-policy interests in Haiti did so as unmarked transvestites. This cast of quality-crossing characters was dispatched to Haiti at the eleventh hour to avert a U.S. invasion of the country. American bombers were enroute to Haiti when President Clinton called off the invasion. It was Carter who convinced representatives of the de facto Cédras government to accept a "soft landing."

My claim that Carter, Powell, and Nunn are unmarked transvestites is not that they literally dressed as women on this mission, but rather that each of these individuals embodies the quality of crossing. Like transvestites, each in some way signifies both more and less than meets the eye. In this respect, each is beyond representation because each, in different ways, resists description within some dichotomous codes (male or female, Republican or Democrat, black or white, inside or outside). In combination, this diplomatic team affects a U.S. foreign-policy strategy of masquerade toward Haiti.

Jimmy Carter — Beyond Desire and Politics

> Staying within your brief is an antithetical to Jimmy Carter. (Comment on Jimmy Carter's foreign-policy style by an anonymous former Carter official; *New York Times,* September 21, 1994: A9)

When thinking about Carter, a disavowal of desire is among the things one recalls. By disavowing desire, Carter appears as a male in masquerade because he "works to effect a separation between the cause of desire and [himself]" (Doane, 1991: 29). This is illustrated by the statement that Carter made to an interviewer at *Playboy* magazine: "I've looked on a lot of women with lust. I've committed adultery in my heart many times" (quote reproduced in *New York Times,* January 18, 1995: B4). But that is all behind him. That was "when I was young enough to lust" (*Tonight Show,* February 8, 1995). Whether because of age, self-control, or religious conviction, Jimmy Carter appears in the American imaginary not so much as incapable of lust as beyond lust and (because in the American imaginary they are often seen to be interchangeable) as beyond desire. Carter occupies an "outside sex position" (Millot, 1990: 65).

The former president's positioning as beyond desire locates him not only as an unmarked transvestite—as one who serves as an unconscious sign of gender crossing. He also occupies the position of an "unmarked" transsexual—one who "is" the other sex in a presurgical sense and who is therefore beyond sex because of neither sex. As Tim Dean explains, "The example of transsexual identification . . . suggests that male-to-female transvestism or transsexualism represents an identification not with the other sex but with what is beyond gender, *horsexe*" (Dean, 1993: 17).

Carter cannot "stay within his brief" not because of his abundant lust but because briefs do not fit his (non)sex. Carter has symbolically crossed the sex line, so much so that he not only appears not to "have" the phallus, but he occasionally appears to "be" the phallus. Symbolically, he is neither male nor female, masculine nor feminine, and occasionally is mistaken for either sex or gender. He is mistaken as masculine because he was born a man. He is mistaken as feminine because "[f]emininity is fundamentally...the play of masks... it conceals only an absence of 'pure' or 'real' femininity" (Doane commenting on Riviere's work; Doane, 1991: 37). In other words, it is an open secret that Carter's gender—whether masculine or feminine—is but a mask.

Jimmy Carter finds himself in the outsider position regarding politics as well. His unofficial power comes from "the veneer of an office he no longer holds" (Wooten, 1995). With the Carter Center at Emory University functioning as an alternative Department of State, Carter as elder statesperson has crossed over to freelance diplomat. As one political commentator writes, "Carter sees himself as exploiting a special niche, as one who can bring to any situation the authority of his former office and the credibility gained by years of global good works outside official channels, in exile from American politics" (*New York Times*, September 22, 1994).

Because of Carter's outsider status, he is in a position to be all things to all people. As a glowing presidential afterimage, Carter has experienced a political rebirth in recent years. Wrapped up in moral causes that cross over his sex and gender, Carter has intervened in crisis situations such as the Bosnian conflict and the North Korean nuclear crisis, as well as the Haitian elections and the eleventh-hour negotiations to avert a U.S. invasion into Haiti. Again, like an unmarked transvestite/transsexual, Carter is something of a superstar. His position consists of wanting to be All. Whereas the male-to-female transsexual wants to be "all women, more woman than all women" (Millot, 1990: 42), Carter wants to be all diplomats, more diplomat than all diplomats. Transcending politics, Carter aspires to be a universal peacemaker.

Carter made the most of his positions outside desire and politics during the U.S. diplomatic mission to Haiti. As "a detached observer, outsider, in the place of the Other" (ibid., 66), Carter identified with the positions of both the Clinton administration and the Cédras administration. He could "feel himself to be both the one and the other, and even neither" (ibid.). So positioned, Carter used his shame of desire (forceful entry) to U.S. political advantage. He is reported to have told Cédras that he was "ashamed of the United States policy" toward Haiti at the moment that he learned that President Clinton had dispatched the invasion force (*New York Times,* September 22, 1994: A19). Although Carter later told reporters he was only speaking to Cédras about U.S. economic policy (*Newsweek,* October 3, 1994: 38), the effect of his well-timed declaration of shame was to persuade de facto Haitian leaders to sign the agreement that averted the invasion.

General Colin Powell — Beyond Identification

> As for his political views, he remains what a New York media consultant, Deroy Murdock, termed "a riddle wrapped in a mystery inside a uniform." (*New York Times,* February 1, 1995: A8)

General Colin Powell's participation in the U.S. diplomatic mission to Haiti was vital to the United States' self-declared strategy of brinkmanship. As a former chairperson of the Joint Chiefs of Staff and the architect of the Persian Gulf War, he stood for military preparedness and honor. Although he preferred to save Haitian and American lives, he was man enough to use force when necessary. Giving the American body politic a masculine face (thereby symbolically rephallusizing it), Powell suggested to the Haitians that the United States "has" the phallus. In this sense, Powell was the perfect choice to balance Jimmy Carter, a figure who (because he lacks the phallus) often appears to be feminine to his very core. This coupling of Powell and Carter on a diplomatic mission was, as Secretary of State Warren Christopher suggested, "one instance where power has served diplomacy in an absolutely classic way" (White House briefing regarding the agreement reached in Haiti; Federal New Service, September 18, 1994: 4).

Powell's symbolic function as masculine, however, while asserted, could not be proved. One could never be sure just what mystery Powell's uniform veiled because just who Powell was could not be represented. He was, like Carter, another case of a neither/nor. Powell's axis of undecidability at the time of the intervasion concerned political affiliation.

When asked whether he was a Democrat or a Republican, Powell replied, "I will not dodge this question. I will answer it right back, straight-forwardly: I am neither" (*New York Times*, February 1, 1995: A8). He elaborated that during his military career his "entire code of honor said, Don't be political, never show any partisanship, either Democratic or Republican or anything that would suggest politics" (ibid.). Although some may suggest that Powell was simply concealing his partisanship, the general insisted that his political philosophy was evolving. The "fact" about Powell's political identification was that there was nothing to conceal.

Race played a similarly unrepresentable role in Powell's participation in the Haiti mission. As a light-skinned black American, Powell is located on the racial edge of America's hegemonic hue of whiteness. He is popularly consumed by white Americans as not "black enough" to be a threat to the "whiting" of America and by black Americans as not "white enough" to cross over the color line as a traitor to his race.

Powell's race accentuated his political capital on the Haiti mission. Like Carter, here was a man who could sympathize with both sides of the dispute — the whiting-out America and the predominately black Haiti. Whereas Carter's participation symbolically squashed criticism of most of America's morally suspect interests in the invasion, Powell did the same for America's political and racial interests. As a nonpartisan American of African descent, Powell symbolically deflected criticism away from the overtly racist implications of U.S. immigration policy toward Haiti — the enforcement of which some believed was the primary objective of the intervasion.

Senator Sam Nunn — A Sacred Marker

As the French say, there are three sexes — men, women, and clergymen. (Sydney Smith, *Lady Holland's Memoir* [1855]; quoted in Garber, 1992: 210)

The sacred thus finds its place at the heart of the transsexual enigma. (Millot, 1991: 70)

If Jimmy Carter (an unofficial diplomat who at times appears to "be" the phallus) and Colin Powell (an unofficial military man who appears to "have" the phallus) combined to assure a U.S. policy of brinkmanship toward Haiti, why was it necessary to include Senator Sam Nunn on this mission as well? Nunn functioned as an official figure who both joined and separated the symbolic bodies of Carter and Powell by identifying with both in different ways. As a Georgian and a Democrat, Nunn identified with Carter, the former governor of Georgia. As a senator who made his career as a proponent of a strong U.S. military — even when that meant that he made unpopular arguments for increased defense budgets and the reinstatement of the draft — he seemed related to Powell's political body. These identifications should not be overread as alignments with either Carter or Powell. Nunn — like every other member of this diplomatic parade of unmarked transvestites — was a neither/nor whose nonidentity was played out in the role of intermediary. Neither on Carter's side nor Powell's — neither feminine nor masculine, neither female nor male — Nunn's role was to refuse to take sides. Positioned as a middleman (or as his name suggests, maybe also a middlewoman), Nunn functioned as a sacred/celibate marker who both distinguished between Carter and Powell as two sides of U.S. foreign policy (diplomacy and power) and joined them into one indistinguishable figure (a male body in female dress).

Nunn's function as the official third term on the diplomatic mission symbolically invested him with seeing to the mission's overall success — both as a member of the U.S. government and as the guardian of the processes of diplomacy and democracy. The *New York Times* reported that President Clinton "saw Senator Nunn, the chairman of the Senate Armed Services Committee, as someone who could tell Haiti's leaders that strong opposition in Congress [to a U.S.-led invasion] would not necessarily be an obstacle to Mr. Clinton's action" (*New York Times,* September 19, 1994: A4). Whenever Nunn spoke officially about his role on the mission, he confessed his steadfast faith in democracy.

The day after the agreement was reached between the Haitians and the Carter-led diplomatic team, Senator Nunn told reporters:

> I will repeat the point that I made over and over again to the Haitian leadership, and that is that returning one man, even though elected and even though he certainly should and will be returned, is not democracy. Democracy involves institutions. Democracy involves an elected parliament. I hope that the focal point of our foreign policy can be, in addition to returning President Aristide, free and fair elections of a parliament. (News conference concerning Haiti; Federal News Service, September 19, 1994: 7)

Nunn's words to the Haitian leaders were not hollow. As Jimmy Carter noted, "Senator Sam Nunn brought the parliamentary approach to the discussions in their crucial stages" (ibid.). Putting his sacred mark as a hawk in sister's clothes on the process, Nunn ensured that the profane mission goals were accomplished—that a "hard diplomatic and military line" was used to enable a "soft military landing" in Haiti.

With Nunn flanked by Carter and Powell, this diplomatic team collectively performed as a third term in the intervasion discourse. Neither fully marked by Clinton's political agenda nor unmarked by it, this team fell somewhere "*between* the mark and the non-mark." As a "*supplement* of classification, it join[ed] realms, passions, character." In so doing, it "*confuse[d]* meaning, the norm, normality" (Barthes, 1976: 107–9). This is how Roland Barthes describes the neuter. Yet grafted onto the figure of the American body politic that is "dressed" in the flag, neuters and neutrality can never be proved. The effect of the political and symbolic mixing of these three foreign-policy figures with the American body politic was to mask America's castrated body and unmark it as castrated.

The Space of Presidential Masquerade

[T]he transvestite does represent a third space ... even within a psychic economy in which *all* positions are fantasies. (Garber, 1992: 356)

The space of presidential masquerade is this third space of the transvestite/transsexual. In this space, no one can "be" or "have" the phallus; one can only *appear* (not) to "be" or "have" it. The space of presidential masquerade is not a space in which meanings can be guaranteed as they are in a logic of representation (where dichotomous terms or signifiers seem to capture meanings). Nor is it a space of simulation (where truth is in hypercirculation). Rather, in this space of masquerade it is the fake that is in hypercirculation. Here signifiers appear to match up in boundary-crossing ways, in ways that celebrate the apparent absence of the real rather than try to conceal this absence. Mixed figures (a diplomatic parade of unmarked transvestites) affect mixed events (the U.S.-led "intervasion" of Haiti).

We are left with a mixed presidential figure, one whom the press referred to after the Haiti intervasion as "Jimmy Clinton, II" (*New York Times,* September 22, 1994: A19) — a figure who unconsciously appeared in foreign policy dressed as a woman, thereby effectively underscoring America's phallic authority in the Caribbean. This paradoxical result could not be accomplished outside of the space of masquerade, for this is the space in which castration is embraced as a way to escape "the anxiety of phallic loss. The overdetermination of phallic jokes, verbal and visual ... is a manifestation of exactly this strategy of reassurance for anxiety through artifactual overcompensation" (Garber, 1992: 356). There are few better ways to describe the U.S.-led intervasion of Haiti and the combination of diplomatic and military efforts that created it.

The United States emerged from the intervasion of Haiti as a mixed foreign-policy figure because it overcame its castration anxiety in the Caribbean by embracing castration. As an already castrated figure, it has nothing left to lose and, therefore, nothing left to fear losing. Now positioned beyond castration anxiety, the United States in male masquerade appears to be more hegemonic than all hegemonic states. This is the position George Bush claimed for it in the New World Order, but one he failed to achieve with respect to the Caribbean because he inscribed U.S. hegemonic subjectivity in hysterical hypermasculine terms when in fact it could have more effectively been inscribed in the "kinder, gentler" ways of which Bush spoke, but which he was not "man" enough to carry out. Bill (Jimmy) Clinton, in contrast, through his mixed policy toward Haiti, has managed to lay a different kind of claim to U.S. masculine hegemonic subjectivity by queering U.S. foreign policy toward the Caribbean and reinscribing the subjectivity of the American body politic as a transvestite/transsexual. No longer does the United States announce its motto as "Speak softly and carry a big stick"; rather, the U.S. slogan for its Caribbean policy after the Cold War is "You can't assume that just because I'm in a dress I left my dick at home" (anonymous lesbian quoted in ibid., 147).

7. America's Queer Accessory

If, as Roland Barthes wrote, "what is told is always in the telling" (Barthes, 1974: 213), what is in my telling of this fable of America's quest for a straight, masculine hegemonic identity in a "post-phallic" era?

The way this question is traditionally engaged in a conclusion is to approach the story just told as one doing a Barthesian first reading. A first reading of my story would read what has already been read, what readers recognize as the story's seemingly stable content that they can identify with (if only on the level of laughter). Following the form of a first reading, this concluding chapter would simply summarize the episodes already elaborated in the book. It would go something like this...

I tell a story about the American body politic's symbolic castration resulting from its encounter with Castro's Cuba and subsequently recount the various refigurations this body has deployed to rephallusize itself—denial, successful simulation, failed simulation, and dissimulation. In this post-phallic era in which America does not have the phallus but always hopes to have it (again), all manner of compensatory strategies are explored. Paradoxically, the American body politic ultimately reasserts its claim to straight, masculine hegemonic identity by queering its phallic endowment. So long as the queer content of America's rephallusization strategies remain unconscious—as they did in President Bush's transvestite encirclement of Panama and in President Clinton's sex/gender/sexuality crossing of the American body politic under the sign of presidential masquerade—these strategies allow the American body politic to "have it" (the phallus) any way it can get it. On this first reading, it does not matter if America's phallus is real or fake or even queer. All that matters is that the American body politic emerges at the end of this story as rephallusized. So refigured, it can claim its place in the New World Order as a regional and global hegemon.

This first reading—like any first reading—accepts the terms in which the characters in this tale have been presented so far. The American body politic—our male lead—is accepted as a figure who had the phallus but lost it and went on to (re)cover its losses in any way it could. The Caribbean Sea/See/Screen—our supporting actress—remains that mysterious woman in the background without whom this story would not have been possible but who (like so many storybook women) is the root cause of all the trouble (the) male character experiences. Had she remained calm and not meddled with America's masterful masculinity, this turbulent tale could have been avoided. The conclusion to be drawn from this first reading does not recast these characters. America remains the caped crusader and the Caribbean Sea/See/Screen is his damsel in distress, even if what the American body politic rescues in a "post-phallic" era is itself (as hegemonic and narcissistically loved).

This readerly conclusion tells us a lot. It tells us what happened to whom, when, and where. Put differently, it summarizes the denotative content of my connotatively configured tale. But if we stop the story here and content ourself with this first denotative reading, we fail to address (or more interestingly, to redress) the Barthesian question, what is in the telling of this tale? For, even though this first reading does not ignore the connotative content of this story, it too readily accepts the seemingly stable terms in which this story appears to have been told. If we are to consider the Barthesian question, we must push on to destabilize this narrative once more. To do this, we must perform a rereading of this story.

A rereading of the story approaches the text as writerly rather than readerly. It does not seek out the already read to read it again as we read it before. Readers of writerly texts do not look to a text to perform an identification between themselves and some seemingly stable aspects of the text because, from a writerly perspective, every rereading is an active coproducing or coauthoring of a text by its reader/writer. In this sense, there is no stable content to a text. Writerly rereadings instead seek to interpret a text, "to appreciate what *plural* constitutes it" (Barthes, 1974: 5; emphasis in original). One way to grasp the plural that constitutes a text is to defamiliarize the text from the reader. This does not mean that no identification takes place between the writerly rereader and the text, for that would make the text unintelligible. Instead, there is a shift in emphasis from reading the seemingly stable denotative content of the text to rereading the pluralizing, less familiar connotative content of the text. It is connotation that unleashes the figurative/figural aspects of the text, that painstakingly introduces a deliberate static into any denotative reading. It is connotation that moves the reader from communication (reading the already read) to countercommunication (seeking out what makes this denotative, first reading possible).

In my writerly conclusion to my story, I reread the story I have told about U.S. hegemony through the deliberate static I have introduced into America's own tale about its quest for straight, hegemonic masculinity in the Caribbean. This deliberate static or countercommunication is a figuratively transfigured plural that makes my story possible—an American body politic that straps on a *necessarily* fake and queer dildo in order for it to appear to be hegemonically masculine. My writerly conclusion defamiliarizes and then reinvents the text I have written by highlighting the theoretical importance of my pairing of hegemony and de(tachable)phallusization through a performative reengagement of the American body in pieces with another body in pieces—a few stray lines of Adrienne Rich's poem "Transcendental

Etude." Rich's poem tells the partialized and then accessorized American body politic too much. It tells this body what is in the telling of its own Caribbean tale and what is in my retelling of this tale piece by piece.

A Whole New Hegemony Beginning Here

> But in fact we were always like this,
> rootless, dismembered: knowing it makes the difference.
>
> *(Rich, 1978: 75)*

The story I tell of the American body politic's castrating encounter with Castro's Cuba and its subsequent strategies of rephallusization is a false telling. This is not because these connotatively configured events did not happen. They "did." Rather, it is because my initial casting of the American body politic as a phallic figure is "untrue"; for what my story claims the American body politic lost in its encounter with Castro's Cuba is something that it never had, the phallus. In Jacques Lacan's terms, every body is in a sense "post-phallic" because no one can "be" or "have" the phallus. The psychoanalytic positions of "being" (a woman) and "having" (a phallic claim to manhood) can never be achieved. They are positions that subjects regularly attempt to enact. But "both positions of 'having' and 'being' are, in Lacan's terms, finally to be understood as comedic failures that are nevertheless compelled to articulate and enact these repeated impossibilities" (Butler, 1990: 46).

The American body politic's quest for hegemonic masculinity in a "post-phallic" era might be understood as one of these comedic failures. Trying to avoid a conscious queering of its subjectivity by ensuring that it would never "be" the phallus for another subject, the American body politic nevertheless did not "have" the phallus. Although America's encounter with Castro's Cuba (re)affirmed its castration and unleashed a plurality of compensatory strategies to keep

America ignorant of its bodily facts, the American body politic did not lose its phallus in its encounter with Castro's Cuba for it never "had" a phallus to lose. By this logic, its attempts to rephallusize itself through strategies of denial, simulation, and dissimulation necessarily could never succeed. The American body politic could never be wholly hegemonic, at least in the terms it understood wholeness and hegemony. The American body politic, in Rich's terms, was "always like this, rootless, dismembered."

Lacanian psychoanalytic theory reinscribes subjectivity as a performative enactment of nonpositions, of positions never guaranteed by "being" or "having" the phallus. This reinscription is not just interesting because it results in "comedic failures" of phallic subjectivities. More interestingly, it is in these nonpositions—as a non-"being" or non-"having"—that creative and powerful refigurings of subjectivity take place. It is in this third space or nonspace that the subjectivity of the American body politic is reconfigured as "rootless, dismembered," and—paradoxically—hegemonically "whole." This mixed result is made possible by the symbolic location of America. America is located in an imaginary space in which all things can be achieved, even one's sex, gender, and sexuality. "What," asks Tim Dean, "could be more democratic, more essentially American, than a gender that 'can be manipulated at will'?" He concludes, "Drag is as American as apple pie" (Dean, 1993: 2).

The American body politic succeeded in manipulating its "will" only when it entered this third space—a space between "being" and "having," female and male, feminine and masculine. This is the space of the transvestite and the transsexual, and this space is queer because it defies "normalized" standards of sex, sexuality, and subjectivity. Ironically, this nonnormalized queer space is the only "real" space of subjectivity left in the Lacanian psychoanalytic system. Subjectivity becomes not a "being" or a "having" but an *appearing*, whether this is an appearing to "be" or to "have" or an appearing not to "be" or not to "have" the phallus. By appearing not to have the phallus in its intervasion of Haiti, the American body politic laid a queer claim to hegemonic subjectivity—a claim to wholeness made possible by dismemberment.

If membership ("having" the phallus) has its privileges, dismemberment (strapping on a "fake" phallus) appears to have more privileges in a "post-phallic" era. This was the American body politic's symbolic gesture in its intervasion of Haiti. Around its crusader's cloak of red, white, and blue, this body daggered itself with a queer dildo. America's strategic harnessing of queer sexuality re(covered) America's international phallic power by elevating America's "loss" of a functioning penis into a "gain" of a hegemonic phallus.

Strapping on a dildo should not be conflated with strapping on a penis. "[P]enises can only be compared to dildos in the sense that they take up space" (Bright, 1992: 18–19). And, when considering my imagined American body politic, there appears to be nothing authentically penislike about America's dildo—not its color, shape, size, or necessary harness. Rather than as a substitute penis, the dildo might better be thought of as a phallus substitute. This is what Charles Bernheimer implies when he writes, "For a penis to be phallic the blood would have to be drained from it and replaced by an enduring artificial substance. It would have to become a dildo" (Bernheimer, 1992: 111–12). Only in this way can any penile "refractory period" be eliminated, such as the fading and failing simulations of Presidents Reagan and Bush. Only then can the erection of the fake be sustained, as it appears to be under President Clinton.

President Clinton unconsciously refigured the American body politic by symbolically strapping onto it a "fantasy phallus," "an inappropriate object precariously attached to a desiring fantasy [for U.S. hegemonic masculinity], unsupported by any perceptual memory [of 'having' the phallus]" (Bersani and Dutoit, 1985: 69; my insertions). By donning this fantasy phallus, the American body politic both unconsciously acknowledged its castration/lack and overcame it; for, as Bernheimer argues, "The phallus is maleness elevated to the level of universality at the expense of the body's castration" (Bernheimer, 1992: 130).

Unlike the penis that cannot be detached and reattached to the body at/as will, the dildo — because it is both "rootless" and "dismembered" — can. It is the harness that gives the dildo the ability to have it all ways. The harness literally makes the phallus "*no* organ, a property defined by its very *plasticity, transferability,* and *expropriability*" (Butler, 1993: 61; emphasis in original). Because the dildo can be detached from the body (politic), the body (politic) also "can be detached from its phallic burden" (Lamos, 1995: 120). In other words, dismemberment has only privileges (hegemony), no responsibilities (accountability for international actions). Insensitivity is something that comes with strapped-on dildos, for the body "with the strap-on cannot feel any sensation in [its] rubber dildo. Yet this insensitivity permits even greater control and hence heightened phallicism, for the penetrator may remain untouched by the caresses and body of the penetrated" (ibid., 115–16). This seems to be an appropriate description of a masculinized America's relationship to the feminized Caribbean.

By strapping on the dildo, America's body politic also takes power from the dildo's specularity. The display of the fake keeps others guessing about the presence and function of the real. Does America have the "real" phallus or was America "really" symbolically castrated in its foreign policy toward the Caribbean? Alternatively, as I suggest, does some combination of terms — symbolic castration and phallusization — better describe the American body politic? Only America "knows" for sure. The specularity of America's strapped-on dildo returns the question of U.S. phallic power to the other, leaving the other without any "real" basis for drawing conclusions.

But what exactly does America itself "know"? The story just told seems to suggest that the American body politic first thought it had the phallus and then thought it lost the phallus. Although these two pieces of knowledge — "having" and "losing" — are unconscious knowings, they nevertheless make a difference in American foreign policy; for it is these pieces of (non)knowledge that compel the American body politic to deny and defer the knowledge of its castration and to embark on a series of rephallusization strategies "anchored" in/on the Caribbean. This is one sense in which "knowing it makes the difference."

What the American body politic (falsely) knows is that it was castrated by Castro's Cuba, and it compensated for its castration by symbolically strapping on an accessory—a phallic dildo. Once its phallic power was "restored," the American body politic once again could claim its place in the New World Order as straight, masculine, and hegemonically whole. Looking into the Caribbean Sea/See/Screen to support its hegemonic claim, this is the self-image the American body politic narcissistically admires. This is the story the American body politic tells itself, a story that tells us both what the American body politic (falsely) knows (that it had the phallus, lost the phallus, and regained the phallus) and what the American body politic necessarily must not know (that it never "had" the phallus and that the phallus it now wears is queer). This is what is in America's telling of its hegemonic tale.

It is what the American body politic must not know that is in my retelling of this tale. My retelling/rewriting is only possible if I reinscribe the starring characters in this story. The American body politic is twice rewritten—first as a body that never "had" the phallus and second as a body that (re)gained the phallus by strapping on a queer accessory. To remain hegemonic, the American body politic must remain (at least consciously) ignorant of its refigurations.

It is precisely this unconscious nonknowledge that my reinscribed Caribbean Sea/See/Screen shows the American body politic. The Caribbean Sea/See/Screen never appears in my telling of America's hegemonic tale as a passive, reflecting/screening surface. If it had, America's interventions to restabilize this surface would not have been necessary. Instead, the Caribbean Sea/See/Screen makes it first appearance in my story as a whirlpool, as a turbulent surface that resisted showing the American body politic the image of itself it so hopes to see in the Caribbean.

In this writerly conclusion, the Caribbean Sea/See/Screen is recast as not just a troublesome, turbulent woman but as an active agent who neut(e)ralizes American's hegemonic self-image. The Caribbean Sea/See/Screen achieves this neut(e)ralization of American hegemony not—as the American body politic long feared—by refusing to serve as a reflecting/screening surface. Instead, it neut(e)ralizes the American body politic by reflecting/screening back to this body images of itself that it must not see or consciously know exist. What the Caribbean Sea/See/Screen threatens to show to this headless hegemon is the fakeness of its member.

America's queer accessory—the lavender dildo—is reflected/screened for America's viewing by the Caribbean Sea/See/Screen. What America confronts in this image of itself (if it dares to look) is the horror of the visible that reminds it not so much of its "loss" of phallic power in the Caribbean but of what it never had: the phallus. As an always already castrated body, the American body politic sees in the Caribbean Sea/See/Screen that its "reassuring masculinity...is based on castration" (B. Johnson, 1980: 10). To be phallic in a "post-phallic" era, the American body politic must strap on a dildo. But even this accessorizing act does not solve America's hegemonic identity crisis. Even though "the phallus is maleness elevated to the level of universality" (Bernheimer, 1992: 130), there is nothing uniformly universal about "maleness" or "masculinity." They, too, can be refigured and are refigured wearing a "fake" phallus. Colleen Lamos suggests that "if the dildo has anything to reveal, perhaps it is that the phallus is a figure subject to and constructed through substitutions" (Lamos, 1995: 120). What the Caribbean Sea/See/Screen reveals to the American body politic is that its hegemonic wholeness and its idealized sense of manhood are "rooted" on substitutions.

The fakeness of America's member is vital in this writerly rereading. On the one hand, it is the sustained erection of the fake that makes America hegemonically whole in a post-phallic era. America's substitution of a dildo for its faulty penis elevates the American body politic to a place it never before occupied—to the status of a hegemon whose detachable phallus allows it to "have" hegemonic phallic power without having any unwanted burdens of hegemonic responsibility. On the other hand, however, this story of endless substitutions and attachments to the American body in pieces tells us something else—that America's claim to straight, masculine hegemonic subjectivity is "rooted" on a "dismembered" phallus that is also queer. It is only by unconsciously embracing America's symbolic castration and moving into the seems-to space of subjectivity—into the queer space of the transvestite and the transsexual—that the American body politic is rephallusized. This is both an empowering and a disempowering move for the American body politic. Moving into the trans-space of subjectivity is empowering for America because it is the only space in which the American body politic can make a claim to phallic hegemony in a "post-phallic" era. It is a disempowering move for the American body politic, however, because the American body politic "knows" its claim to straight, masculine, phallic hegemonic subjectivity to be staged within a heterosexual matrix of desire. Acting within this heterosexual matrix, the American body politic seems to conduct itself as if the positions of "having" the phallus and "being" the phallus were guaranteed. For the American body politic, this means that it can "have" the phallus so long as a feminized Caribbean Sea/See/Screen will "be" the phallus for it. But these positions are never guaranteed; and, in a "post-phallic" era, they paradoxically *seem* to be guaranteed only when the subject moves out of the heterosexual matrix of desire into the trans(vestite)sexual matrix of desire.

It is America's move into the seems-to space of desire that it desperately hopes to conceal from itself; for its move into this space is not recognized or made conscious in American foreign-policy discourse, and, if made conscious, it would disrupt the claims to straight hegemonic masculinity the American body politic forever seems to be making.

The secret of America's queer member is the surplus (to sexuality and to the dildo) that the Caribbean Sea/See/Screen shows the American body politic. Confronted with this secret, the American body politic is confronted with its own phallic masquerade—a masquerade it "knows" to be straight even though it is (unconsciously) enacted within queer spaces of subjectivity. If the American body politic gazes "knowingly" (i.e., consciously) into the Caribbean Sea/See/Screen in a "post-phallic" era, it is threatened with images of its own queer strategy of phallic substitution. The Caribbean Sea/See/Screen shows the American body politic that its colors do run, that America's red, white, and blue mixed with the blues of the Caribbean Sea/See/Screen to produce lavender—a shocking new hegemonic hue. This new hegemonic hue is shocking to the American body politic because it simultaneously enables America's straight, masculine (re)phallusization and threatens to destabilize it. As Rich puts it, "knowing it makes the difference."

The "difference" that the Caribbean Sea/See/Screen threatens to make the American body politic "know" is what Barbara Johnson calls the "critical difference" (1980). Such a difference "subverts the very idea of identity, infinitely deferring the possibility of adding up the sum of a text's parts or meanings and reaching a totalized, integrated whole" (ibid., 4). America's critical difference is the difference within America's subjectivity—a seemingly straight subjectivity that is constructed through queer strategies. America's critical difference is the difference within itself (queer and straight, non-"normal" and "normal" sexualities) that never allows American subjectivity to coincide with America's imagined image of itself as straight and hegemonically masculine.

My writerly conclusion does not have a storybook ending. It does not claim, for example, that by making the American body politic know too much, the Caribbean region will be liberated from the hegemonic pretensions of its neighbor to the north. "Knowing" does not generally lead to emancipation; rather, it more often incites the subject confronted with "the truth" to embark on even more elaborate strategies of denial. It is likely that the American body politic will do just that. And, as a headless hegemon, this should not be difficult. What form these strategies of denial and deferral will take is unclear. But given America's investment in its hemispheric identity as the "root" of its global hegemonic identity, it is likely that these denials and deferrals will continue to be told through America's Caribbean policy.

Although the Caribbean region does not "live happily ever after" as my story (temporarily) comes to an end, neither does the American body politic. For, although not "liberated" as the sight of America's hegemonic conquest, the Caribbean Sea/See/Screen is also not a passive, powerless playground for America's hegemonic hopes. The Caribbean Sea/See/Screen resists American advances by making America's difference "known" to those who (re)read/(re)view it. The Caribbean Sea/See/Screen offers up the plural, the sexual surplus, that seems to constitute America's hegemonic identity in a "post-phallic" era — America's strapped-on queer dildo.

If we reread what the Caribbean Sea/See/Screen shows us, we find that the American body politic's reassuring sense of hegemonic masculinity is not only based on castration. It is also based on queer compensations. America's queer accessory is an "active and violent indetermination" that makes American hegemonic identity possible in a "post-phallic" era (ibid., 8). In this writerly rereading of American hegemony, queer elements make their appearances as "noise" or "static" that cannot be represented in America's tall tale of its own hegemonic identity. They appear as nonpositions, nondefinitions, nonbeing — as gaps in American identity. Figuratively rereading America's figural gaps is one way to strategically unharness American hegemony.

BIBLIOGRAPHY

American Foreign Policy Current Documents (AFPCD). 1983. Washington, D.C.: U.S. Government Printing Office.

Apter, Emily. 1991. *Feminizing the Fetish: Psychoanalysis and Narrative Obsession in Turn-of-the-Century France*. Ithaca, N.Y.: Cornell University Press.

Ashby, Timothy. 1988. "The Reagan Years." In *The Caribbean after Grenada: Revolution, Conflict, and Democracy*, Scott B. MacDonald, Harald M. Sandstrom, and Paul B. Goodwin Jr., eds., 269–78. New York: Praeger.

Attali, Jacques. 1985. *Noise: The Political Economy of Music*. Translated by Brian Massumi. Minneapolis: University of Minnesota Press.

Balzac, Honoré de. 1974. "Sarrasine." In *S/Z: An Essay* by Roland Barthes, translated by Richard Miller. New York: Hill and Wang.

Barthes, Roland. 1974. *S/Z: An Essay*. Translated by Richard Miller. New York: Hill and Wang.

———. 1976. *Sade, Fourier, Loyola*. Translated by Richard Miller. New York: Hill and Wang.

Baudrillard, Jean. 1983. *Simulations*. Translated by Paul Foss, Paul Patton, and Philip Beitchman. New York: Semiotext(e).

Benítez-Rojo, Antonio. 1992. *The Repeating Island: The Caribbean and the Postmodern Perspective*. Translated by James E. Maraniss. Durham, N.C.: Duke University Press.

Berg, Maggie. 1991. "Luce Irigaray's 'Contradictions': Poststructuralism and Feminism." *Signs: Journal of Women in Culture and Society* 17: 50–70.

Berlant, Lauren. 1991. *The Anatomy of National Fantasy: Hawthorne, Utopia, and Everyday Life*. Chicago: University of Chicago Press.

Berlant, Lauren, and Elizabeth Freeman. 1993. "Queer Nationalities." In *Fear of a Queer Planet: Queer Politics and Social Theory*, Michael Warner, ed., 193–229. Minneapolis: University of Minnesota Press.

Bernheimer, Charles. 1992. "Penile Reference in Phallic Theory." *Differences* 4(1): 116–32.

Bersani, Leo, and Ulysse Dutoit. 1985. *The Forms of Violence: Narrative in Assyrian Art and Modern Culture*. New York: Schocken Books.

Bérubé, Michael, and Gerald Graff. 1994. "Regulations for Literary Criticism in the 1990s." Teachers for a Democratic Culture.

Black, George. 1988. *The Good Neighbor: How the United States Wrote the History of Central America and the Caribbean*. New York: Pantheon.

Bonsal, Philip W. 1971. *Cuba, Castro, and the United States*. Pittsburgh: University of Pittsburgh Press.

Bright, Susie. 1992. *Susie Sexpert's Lesbian Sex World*. Pittsburgh: Cleis Press.

Bush, George. 1989. "Freedom and World Prosperity." *Current Policy* 1210 (September 27): 1–3.

———. 1990. "U.S. Military Action in Panama." *American Foreign Policy Current Documents 1989*. Washington, D.C.: U.S. Department of State.

Butler, Judith. 1990. *Gender Trouble: Feminism and the Subversion of Identity*. New York: Routledge.

———. 1993. *Bodies that Matter: On the Discursive Limits of "Sex."* New York: Routledge.

Cannon, Lou. 1982. *Reagan*. New York: G. P. Putnam's Sons.

Chayes, Abram. 1974. *The Cuban Missile Crisis*. New York: Oxford University Press.

Congressional Quarterly Weekly Report. 1990. January 6: 43–44.

Dean, Tim. 1993. "Transsexual Identification, Gender Performance Theory, and the Politics of the Real." *Literature and Psychology* 39(4): 1–27.

Debrix, François. 1999. *Re-envisioning Peacekeeping: The United Nations and the Mobilization of Ideology*. Minneapolis: University of Minnesota Press.

Destler, I. M. 1983. "The Evolution of Reagan Foreign Policy." In *The Reagan Presidency: An Early Assessment*, Fred I. Greenstein, ed., 117–58. Baltimore: Johns Hopkins University Press.

DiPiero, Thomas. 1991. "The Patriarch Is Not (Just) a Man." *Camera Obscura* 25–26: 101–24.

Doane, Mary Ann. 1991. *Femmes Fatales: Feminism, Film Theory, Psychoanalysis*. New York: Routledge.

Domingues, Jorge I. 1989. *To Make a World Safe for Revolution: Cuba's Foreign Policy*. Cambridge: Harvard University Press.

Doty, Alexander. 1993. *Making Things Perfectly Queer: Interpreting Mass Culture.* Minneapolis: University of Minnesota Press.

Dugger, Ronnie. 1983. *On Reagan: The Man and His Presidency.* New York: McGraw-Hill.

Dumbrell, John. 1997. *American Foreign Policy: Carter to Clinton.* London: MacMillan.

Dunn, Peter M., and Bruce W. Watson. 1985. *American Intervention in Grenada: The Implications of Operation "Urgent Fury."* Boulder, Colo.: Westview Press.

Dyer, Richard. 1988. "White." *Screen* 29 (autumn): 44–64.

Eagleburger, Lawrence. 1989a. "The Case against Panama's Noriega." *Current Policy* 1222 (August 31): 1–6.

———. 1989b. "The OAS and the Crisis in Panama." *Current Policy* 1205 (August 24): 1–3.

Edelman, Murry. 1988. *Constructing the Political Spectacle.* Chicago: University of Chicago Press.

Eisenhower, Dwight D. 1959. *Public Papers of the President, 1959.* Washington, D.C.: U.S. Government Printing Office.

Elshtain, Jean Bethke. 1987. *Women and War.* New York: Basic Books.

Erickson, Paul D. 1985. *Reagan Speaks: The Making of an American Myth.* New York: New York University Press.

Events in Panama. 1989. "Joint Hearings before the Committee on Armed Services and the Select Committee on Intelligence." United States Senate (October 6 and 17 and December 22, 1989). Washington, D.C.: U.S. Government Printing Office.

Falk, Pamela S. 1987. *Cuban Foreign Policy: Caribbean Tempest.* Lexington, Mass.: Lexington.

Foreign Relations of the United States (FRUS). Various years. Washington, D.C.: U.S. Government Printing Office.

Freud, Sigmund. 1984. "Mourning and Melancholia." In *On Metapsychology: The Theory of Psychoanalysis,* vol. 2. London: Penguin.

Garber, Marjorie. 1992. *Vested Interests: Cross-Dressing and Cultural Anxiety.* New York: Routledge.

Geyelin, Philip. 1966. *Lyndon B. Johnson and the World.* London: Pall Mall.

Geyer, Georgie Anne. 1993. *Guerrilla Prince: The Untold Story of Fidel Castro.* Kansas City, Kans.: Andrews and McMeel.

Goldman, Eric F. 1968. *The Tragedy of Lyndon Johnson.* London: MacDonald.

Gosse, Van. 1993. *Where the Boys Are: Cuba, Cold War America and the Making of a New Left.* New York: Verso.

Grosz, Elizabeth. 1995. *Space, Time, and Perversion.* New York: Routledge.

Hennessy, Rosemary. 1993. "Queer Theory." *Signs* 18 (4): 964–79.

Heren, Louis. 1970. *No Hail, No Farewell.* London: Weidenfeld and Nicolson.

Hersh, Seymour. 1983. "The Price of Power: Kissinger, Nixon and Chile." *Atlantic* (December): 31–58.

Howell, Amanda. 1996. "Lost Boys and Angry Ghouls: Vietnam's Undead." *Genders* 23: 297–334.

Irigaray, Luce. 1985a. *Speculum of the Other Woman.* Translated by Gillian C. Gill. Ithaca, N.Y.: Cornell University Press.

———. 1985b. *this sex which is not one.* Translated by Catherine Porter. Ithaca, N.Y.: Cornell University Press.

Jackson, D. Bruce. 1969. *Castro, the Kremlin, and Communism in Latin America.* Baltimore: Johns Hopkins University Press.

Johnson, Barbara. 1980. *The Critical Difference: Essays in the Contemporary Rhetoric of Reading.* Baltimore: Johns Hopkins University Press.

Johnson, Lyndon B. 1966. *Public Papers of the President, 1965.* Washington, D.C.: U.S. Government Printing Office.

———. 1971. *The Vantage Point: Perspectives of the Presidency 1963–1969.* London: Weidenfeld and Nicolson.

Kearns, Doris. 1976. *Lyndon Johnson and the American Dream.* London: André Deutsch.

Kegley, Charles W., Jr., and Eugene R. Wittkopf. 1997. *World Politics: Trend and Transformation.* 6th ed. New York: St. Martin's Press.

Kennedy, John F. 1961. *Public Papers of the President, 1959.* Washington, D.C.: U.S. Government Printing Office.

Kenworthy, Eldon. 1995. *America/Americas: Myth in the Making of U.S. Policy toward Latin America.* University Park, Pa.: Pennsylvania State University Press.

Kirby, Lynne. 1988. "Male Hysteria and Early Cinema." *Camera Obscura* 17: 115–31.

Kirkpatrick, Jeane J. 1983. *The Reagan Phenomenon—and Other Speeches on Foreign Policy.* Washington, D.C.: American Enterprise Institute for Public Policy Research.

Kozak, Michael G. 1989. "Panama Canal: The Strategic Dimension." *Current Policy* 1205 (August 24): 1–3.

Kraus, Sidney, ed. 1979. *The Great Debates: Carter vs. Ford, 1976.* Bloomington: Indiana University Press.

Kryzanek, Michael J. 1985. *U.S.–Latin American Relations.* New York: Praeger.

Lacan, Jacques. 1985. "The Meaning of the Phallus." In *Feminine Sexuality: Jacques Lacan and the école freudienne,* Juliet Mitchell and Jacqueline Rose, eds., Jacqueline Rose, trans. New York: Norton.

Lamos, Colleen. 1995. "Taking on the Phallus." In *Lesbian Erotics,* Karla Jay, ed., 101–24. New York: New York University Press.

Langley, Lester D. 1968. *The Cuban Policy of the United States: A Brief History.* New York: John Wiley and Sons.

LaFeber, Walter. 1994. *The American Age: United States Foreign Policy at Home and Abroad.* New York: Norton.

Lash, Christopher. 1991. *The Culture of Narcissism: American Life in an Age of Diminishing Expectations.* New York: Norton.

Leogrande, William M. 1997. "Enemies Evermore: US Policy toward Cuba after Helms-Burton." *Journal of Latin American Studies* 29: 211–21.

Lowenthal, Abraham F. 1972. *The Dominican Intervention.* Cambridge: Harvard University Press.

Mackinder, Halford. 1895. "Modern Geography, German and English." *Geographical Journal* 6: 367–79.

Matthews, Herbert L. 1961. *The Cuban Story.* New York: George Braziller.

Millot, Catherine. 1990. *Horsexe: Essay on Transsexuality.* Translated by Kenneth Hylton. New York: Autonomedia.

Moi, Toril. 1985. *Sexual/Textual Politics: Feminist Literary Theory.* London: Methuen.

Morton, Brian. 1990. "And Just Why Did We Invade Panama?" *Dissent* 37: 148–50.

Noriega, Manuel. 1989. Statements quoted by Foreign Broadcast Information Service, May 9, 1989, 40–41.

Pastor, Robert. 1982. "Sinking in the Caribbean Basin." *Foreign Policy* 60 (summer): 1038–58.

———. 1988. "The Invasion of Grenada: A Pre- and Post-Mortem." In *The Carribean after Grenada: Revolution, Conflict, and Democracy,* Scott B. MacDonald, Harald M. Sandstrom, and Paul B. Goodwin, Jr., eds., 87–105. New York: Praeger.

———. 1990. "The United States and the Grenada Revolution: Who Pushed First and Why?" In *A Revolution Aborted: The Lessons of Grenada,* Jorge Heine, ed., 181–214. Pittsburgh: Pittsburgh University Press.

———. 1992. *Whirlpool: U.S. Foreign Policy toward Latin America and the Caribbean.* Princeton, N.J.: Princeton University Press.

Public Papers of the President: Ronald Reagan (PPPRR). Various years. Washington, D.C.: U.S. Government Printing Office.

Rabe, Stephen G. 1988. *Eisenhower and Latin America: The Foreign Policy of Anticommunism.* Chapel Hill: University of North Carolina Press.

Reagan, Ronald. Various years 1980–88. *Public Papers of the President: Ronald Reagan.* Washington, D.C.: U.S. Government Printing Office.

———. 1990. *An American Life*. New York: Simon and Schuster.

Reagan, Ronald, with Richard G. Hubler. 1965. *My Early Life; or, Where's the Rest of Me?* London: Sidgwick and Jackson.

Rich, Adrienne. 1978. *The Dream of a Common Language: Poems 1974–1977*. New York: Norton.

Riviere, Joan. 1929. "Womanliness as a Masquerade." *International Journal of Psychoanalysis* 10: 303–13.

Rogin, Michael. 1987. *Ronald Reagan, the Movie*. Berkeley: University of California Press.

Ronfeldt, David. 1983. *Geopolitics, Security, and U.S. Strategy in the Caribbean Basin*. Santa Monica, Calif.: Rand.

Rubenstein, Diane. 1991. "This Is Not a President: Baudrillard, Bush, and Enchanted Simulation." In *The Hysterical Male: New Feminist Theory*, Arthur Kroker and Marilouise Kroker, eds., 253–65. New York: St. Martin's Press.

———. 1993. "Oliver North and the Lying Nose." In *Rhetorical Republics: Governing Representations in American Politics*, Fredrick Dolan and Thomas Dumm, eds., 97–120. Amherst: University of Massachusetts Press.

———. In progress. *Baudrillard Goes to Washington*.

Safford, Jeffery J. 1980. "The Nixon–Castro Meeting of 19 April 1959." *Diplomatic History* 4(4): 426–31.

Salinger, Pierre. 1966. *With Kennedy*. London: Jonathan Cape.

Scarry, Elain. 1985. *The Body in Pain: The Making and Unmaking of the World*. New York: Oxford University Press.

Schlesinger, Arthur M., Jr. 1965. *A Thousand Days: John F. Kennedy in the White House*. New York: Fawcett Premier.

Schor, Namoi. 1989. "This Essentialism Which Is Not One: Coming to Grips with Irigaray." *Differences* 1(2): 38–58.

Selbin, Eric. 1993. *Modern Latin American Revolutions*. Boulder, Colo.: Westview Press.

Serres, Michel. 1987. *L'hermaphrodite: Sarrasine sculpteur*. Flammarion.

Simons, Geoff. 1996. *Cuba: From Conquistador to Castro*. London: MacMillan.

Speakes, Larry, with R. Pack. 1988. *Speaking Out: Inside the Reagan White House*. New York: Scribner's.

Thorndike, Tony. 1989. "Grenada." In *Intervention in the 1980s: U.S. Foreign Policy in the Third World*, Peter J. Schraeder, ed., 249–63. Boulder, Colo.: Lynne Rienner.

Tuathail, Gearóid Ó. 1996. *Critical Geopolitics: The Politics of Writing Global Space*. Minneapolis: University of Minnesota Press.

Walker, William O., III. 1994. "Mixing the Sweet with the Sour: Kennedy, Johnson, and Latin America." In *The Diplomacy of the Crucial Decade: American Foreign Relations During the 1960s,* Diana B. Kunz, ed., 42–79. New York: Columbia University Press.

Walters, Suzanne Danuta. 1996. "From Here to Queer: Radical Feminism, Postmodernism, and the Lesbian Menace (or Why Can't a Woman Be More like a Fag?)." *Signs* 21(4): 830–69.

Warner, Michael. 1993. "Introduction." In *Fear of a Queer Planet: Queer Politics and Social Theory,* Michael Warner, ed., vii–xxxi. Minneapolis: University of Minnesota Press.

Weber, Cynthia. 1995a. "Dissimulating Intervention: A Reading of the U.S.-Led Intervention into Haiti." *Alternatives* 20: 265–77.

———. 1995b. *Simulating Sovereignty: Intervention, the State, and Symbolic Exchange.* Cambridge: Cambridge University Press.

Weldes, Jutta, and Diana Saco. 1996. "Making State Action Possible: The United States and the Discursive Construction of 'The Cuban Problem.' " *Millennium* 25(2): 361–95.

Whitford, Margaret. 1991. *Luce Irigaray: Philosophy in the Feminine.* London: Routledge.

Wiarda, Howard J. 1975. *Dictatorship, Development and Disintegration: Politics and Social Change in the Dominican Republic.* Cambridge, Mass.: Xerox University Microfilms.

Wiarda, Howard J., and Michael J. Kryzanek. 1982. *The Dominican Republic: A Caribbean Crucible.* 2d ed. Boulder, Colo.: Westview Press.

Wills, Gary. 1987. *Reagan's America: Innocents at Home.* New York: Doubleday.

Wolf, John S. 1989. "UN Program Coordination and Narcotics Control." *Current Policy* 1219 (October 17): 1–2.

Wooten, Jim. 1995. "The Conciliator." *New York Times Magazine,* January 29.

INDEX

United Nations, 111, 112, 113–16;
as lack, 114–15; forces, 107; General Assembly, 112; Resolution 940, 113, 115; Security Council, 113

Vietnam, 5, 26, 42–44, 51, 52, 53, 62, 64, 73, 80, 111, 112; and horror films, 49–50; syndrome, 62, 111

Virgin Islands, 65

war on drugs, 95–97
Watergate crisis, 60–61
whiteness, 6, 49; as hegemonic hue, 122

Yugoslavia, 115

Cynthia Weber is associate professor of political science at Purdue University. She has held visiting appointments at the University of Southern California and the University of Wales, Aberystwyth. Weber is the author of *Simulating Sovereignty* and coeditor (with Thomas Biersteker) of *State Sovereignty as Social Construct*.